MW00624785

The Word Made Flesh for Us

"The Elizabethan era was a period of significant controversy in the Protestant Church of England. As the present edition of Book V of Richard Hooker's *Laws* attests, the controversy between what we would today call "Anglicans" and "Presbyterians" was, in many respects, a debate internal to the Reformed tradition about how best to apply shared principles of Reformed Christology and sacramental theology to questions about the church's order and worship. The Davenant Press is once again to be commended for making a work of great historical and theological interest available to a wider audience in a readable and affordable edition."

—SCOTT SWAIN
James Woodrow Hassell Professor of Systematic Theology, Reformed Theological Seminary

"Davenant Press' modernizations of Richard Hooker's *Laws of Ecclesiastical Polity* are essential reading for ministers and lay people. In this volume, Hooker's Christology has clear resonances of John Calvin and his work on the two natures of Christ is masterful. His treatment of the necessity of the sacraments is a treasure for anyone seeking doctrinal clarity from one of the leading reformed English scholars of the late sixteenth century. Anglican readers will be especially interested in Hooker's defense of the Rite of Confirmation and will draw conclusions about the value of Confirmation in our modern liturgical order. Littlejohn and Timmis have gifted us with the rediscovery of Richard Hooker's wisdom, freshly accessible to modern readers."

—JULIAN DOBBS

Diocesan Bishop of the Anglican Diocese of the Living Word

"Richard Hooker's towering Elizabethan prose, and the challenge of finding an affordable copy, has rendered his work doubly difficult to access. This new translation of his sacramental theology from selected passages of Book Five of the *Laws* overcomes both impediments. The translators put Hooker's Elizabethan rhetorical style and idiom into dynamic and contemporary English without losing any of the original genius. Hooker's sacramental theological vision of how God is in Christ, and how Christ is in us, sings into a luminous modern translation. It offers an invaluable devotional and ecumenical resource for all Christians keen to retrieve the riches of their tradition. It ensures that the past still speaks to us, and that Hooker's vision will not pass away as in a dream."

—PAUL DOMINIAK

Senior Tutor, Jesus College Cambridge

"In the contested terrain of post-Reformation theology, the work of Richard Hooker in his *Laws of Ecclesiastical Polity* serves as a significant landmark. Its accounts of Christology and of the sacraments are particularly noteworthy: scripturally resourced, contextually aware, and carefully argued, they articulate a Reformed yet irenic position that not only spoke powerfully to his own time but will also repay careful study today. For this reason, it is a delight to see published in the present volume a new edition of these compelling sections of Hooker's magisterial work. There is much here to ponder and engage."

—PAUL T. NIMMO
King's Chair of Systematic Theology, University of Aberdeen

"*The Word Made Flesh For Us* is a wonderful modernization of Richard Hooker's sixteenth century classic that somehow succeeds in making the work more accessible even as it preserves the breviloquence of its English prose. The editors' choice to focus on Christology and the sacraments is inspired: there is an obvious connection between the hypostatic union (God was in Christ), the mystical union (Christ is in us), and the sacraments (divinely ordained means for cementing this union). Moreover, with its conceptual distinctions and logical inferences, Hooker's Christology is a veritable masterclass in theology that is as analytic as it is orthodox."

—KEVIN VANHOOZER
Research Professor of Systematic Theology, Trinity Evangelical Divinity School

"Brad Littlejohn and Patrick Timmis present a readable and lucid modernization of one of the key sections of the fifth book of *The Laws of Ecclesiastical Polity*. This is a most welcome republication from one of the most learned and most irenic theologians of the Reformation period."

—HANS BOERSMA
Nashotah House Theological Seminary

The Word Made Flesh for Us

The Word Made Flesh for Us

Selections from the fifth book of
Of the Laws of Ecclesiastical Polity

Richard Hooker

Modernized and edited by
BRAD LITTLEJOHN & PATRICK TIMMIS
with Brian Marr

Davenant Press 2024

ISBN-13: 978-1-949716-33-7
ISBN-10: 1-949716-33-3

Front cover image: Peter Horree/Alamy Stock Photo
Cover design and typesetting by
Rachel Rosales, Orange Peel Design
Proofread by Mikael Good

RICHARD HOOKER
by Wenceslaus Hollar

Table of Contents

Introduction

This volume marks the seventh publication in our ongoing project to modernize the works of the great English theologian Richard Hooker. The first four, each slender volumes of 100–150 pages, covered the opening sections of his masterpiece, *The Laws of Ecclesiastical Polity*. In 2019 we then collated these into a single larger volume encompassing the Preface–Book IV of the *Laws*, which in earlier editions have traditionally been bound together as "Volume 1." Thereafter, we took a long hiatus, as other life commitments constantly impeded further progress, although, in 2022, we were able to put out an edition of Hooker's masterful little *Learned Discourse on Justification*. Finally, thanks to the energy and dedication of my new friend Patrick Timmis, we resumed work on the main project, focusing on critical sections of Book V, originally published in 1597. The volume before you today represents the firstfruits of that renewed effort, which hopefully will continue over the coming years to include the rest of Book V, along with Books VI–VIII.

The paragraph above, however, may raise more questions than it answers. Some readers may be new to Richard Hooker altogether. Indeed, our hope is that this present volume, covering as it does central doctrines of the Christian faith of interest to all Protestants—indeed, all Christians—will find many readers far outside the narrow world of Hooker enthusiasts, and outside the Anglican Communion. Other readers may know Hooker's name, but understand little of the *Laws*, why he wrote it, and why it still matters today. Most will wonder what we mean by a "modernization" and why it is necessary. I will seek to answer all of these questions briefly in what follows. Faithful readers of earlier volumes may happily skip this review material, but may still be curious to know more about Book V, and why it is that the present volume skipped right to Chapter 50, instead of starting with Chapter 1. Some readers may not be especially interested in either Hooker or the *Laws*, but yet be keenly interested in the subject: the great mystery of Christ's incarnation, his mystical union with his people, and our participation in him by means of the sacraments. The last part of this introduction, then, will say a bit about these topics, and how to map Hooker's own contribution to them in relation to the minefield of sixteenth-century debates around these doctrines.

Who Was Richard Hooker?[1]

Richard Hooker is a name little known today outside of the Anglican tradition, and less and less even within it. His works, once standard reading for any educated Englishman, have receded far into our cultural rearview mirror, increasingly unreadable and seemingly obsolete in our postmodern age. But they are, as I hope you will find, nearly as relevant today as when they were first penned, and as worthy of our attention as the other literary monuments of the Elizabethan Golden Age.

Hooker wrote in the 1590s, that high tide of Elizabethan intellectual and literary culture which defined the shape of our language and culture right down to the present. While Hooker was in London drafting his *Laws*, Shakespeare was just on the opposite bank of the Thames writing *The Taming of the Shrew*, and Spenser had just returned to Ireland after coming to London to publish and promote his *Faerie Queene*. Francis Bacon was a leading advisor at court, just beginning his literary career. Like these other men, the scale of Hook-

---

1. For a fuller introduction, see Brad Littlejohn, *Richard Hooker: A Companion to His Life and Work* (Eugene: Cascade, 2015).

er's achievement looms up out of the relative mediocrity of his sixteenth-century predecessors with a suddenness that can baffle the historian. Stanley Archer observes, "It is no more possible to account for Hooker's achievement than for those of Shakespeare and Milton, Spenser and Bacon."[2]

What was this achievement? It consists chiefly (though certainly not solely) in Hooker's *Laws of Ecclesiastical Polity*, which ranks alongside the greatest productions of the sixteenth-century Reformation. Indeed, though merely a quiet and unassuming scholar rather than a visionary church leader like Luther and Calvin, Hooker deserves mention in their company for the clarity and timeliness of this theological vision, without whose insights Protestant theology would be forever impoverished. Of course, although Hooker left a legacy from which all Protestants can profit, he is particularly known as the theologian of Anglicanism, or perhaps even its "inventor."[3] Hooker, of course, would have been surprised to hear that there was any such "ism," and he certainly did not knowingly write in defense of it. He wrote rather, as the haunting opening lines of the *Laws* make clear, in defense of the Church

2. Stanley Archer, *Richard Hooker* (Boston: Twayne, 1983), 1.

3. Peter Lake, *Anglicans and Puritans? Presbyterianism and English Conformist Thought from Whitgift to Hooker* (London: Unwin Hyman, 1988), 227.

of England, as it had been established in the reign of Queen Elizabeth I. To understand the man and his work, we must understand the church that he so deeply loved.

A Contested "Middle Way"

Although the Protestant Reformation provoked fierce conflict wherever it broke out, the English Reformation is notorious for being particularly chaotic. Beginning with Henry VIII's fitful and inconstant reformation, prompted more by dynastic and fiscal concerns than theological convictions, the Church of England lurched, in just a fifteen-year period, through at least four distinct phases. In 1546 it was autonomous from Rome but still traditionalist in its doctrine and practice. It then witnessed first a thoroughgoing embrace of Reformed theology and rapid reformation of worship under Edward VI, then a violent Roman Catholic counter-Reformation under Queen Mary, and finally Elizabeth I's imposition of a moderate Protestantism that owed much to Melanchthonian Lutheranism, but which soon provoked a Puritan backlash.

Richard Hooker was born in the bloodiest and most tumultuous phase of this whole bloody and tumultuous story, sometime in late 1553 or early 1554 in Heavitree, a village on the outskirts of Exeter in southwest England—then as now, a prosperous port and a cathedral city. His family were among those who had embraced Protestant doctrines during the time of Edward, and indeed his uncle John was well-connected to key Reformed leaders. The year 1554, however, was not the best time to have such connections. Queen Mary (known to history not unreasonably as "Bloody Mary" for her martyrdom of hundreds of Protestants) had just ascended the throne on the boy-king's death, and was determined to reverse the rapid progress the Reformation had made in England over the past few years. Fortunately for the Hooker family, the Protestant cause did not have to wait long for a dramatic change of fortunes. The sudden death of Mary in late 1558 and accession of the firmly Protestant Queen Elizabeth struck contemporary Protestants as a great act of divine deliverance, and it is difficult for us, looking back on the complexities and compromises of Elizabeth's policies with a historian's eye, to understand just how fervently many of her Protestant subjects reverenced her.

Elizabeth's accession brought the exiled English Protestants hastening home, but the delicate work of hammering out a contested "middle way" was just beginning. In the early years of the Elizabethan Settlement, all of Elizabeth's bishops expected further reformation to move forward in due course, once the dust had settled from the chaos of the recent violent transitions. Elizabeth herself, however, seems to have genuinely favored a more ceremonial mode of worship, and feared the religious radicalism that she attributed to the two-hour-long sermons favored by more zealous Reformers. Besides, the maintenance of some outward trappings of the old medieval religion (whether it be the threefold order of bishops, priests, and deacons, the special vestments worn by priests while celebrating the liturgy, or the retention of ceremonies like confirmation) was, Elizabeth realized, politically desirable. After all, the mere accession of a Protestant monarch had hardly converted the whole kingdom to the new Reformed faith; many thousands of closet Catholics, some among the high nobility, remained throughout the realm, their loyalty to the new regime uncertain. By retaining many forms of worship familiar to them, Elizabeth deemed, she could make their outward conformity easier and reduce the risk of rebellions or conspiracies—ever-present threats throughout her long reign.

There's an old maxim that says, "You can please some of the people all of the time, or you can please all of the people some of the time. But you can't please all of the people all of the time." Alas, so it was for Elizabeth. Working hard to reduce the threat of rebellion from crypto-Catholics, she increasingly earned the ire of more advanced

Protestants, later known to history as "Puritans." Although most Protestant leaders, at home and abroad, agreed that the disputed ceremonies were *adiaphora* or "things indifferent," many pastors thought they could be spiritually dangerous for weaker consciences struggling to leave medieval religion behind.

By enforcing and defending the Queen's demands for uniformity, the bishops quickly found themselves vilified by some of the more radical Puritans, who began to call for an overhaul of the whole system of church government along broadly presbyterian lines. A young Cambridge don named Thomas Cartwright had first begun to outline these ideas in a series of lectures in 1569–70, but they entered the public eye with the publication of the incendiary *Admonition to Parliament* in 1572 by two of his younger disciples, John Field and Thomas Wilcox. This document, ostensibly addressed to Parliament, brazenly declared, "We in England are so far off from having a church rightly reformed, according to the prescript of God's word, that as yet we are not come to the outward face of the same,"[4] and called for the establishment of presbyterian government, along with other major reforms. The

---

4. W. H. Frere and C. E. Douglas, eds., *Puritan Manifestoes: A Study of the Origin of the Puritan Revolt* (London: SPCK, 1907).

pamphlet was suppressed by the authorities, but still traveled far and wide, creating a sensation.[5]

A tedious but heated literary battle ensued over the following five years between Cartwright (now in exile in Holland) and John Whitgift, Master of Trinity College, Cambridge and the future Archbishop of Canterbury. Despite the frequently trivial nature of the issues (for instance, where in the church the minister should stand at certain points in the service), profound differences in ecclesiology lay under the surface, and the interaction generated heated polemics, especially from the younger Cartwright.

Puritans like Cartwright began to insist, in terms perhaps familiar enough to us today but out of step with the early Protestant Reformers, that the Bible was the sole standard for liturgy and church government, and that any church failing to radically reform itself in conformity to Scripture alone was unworthy of the name of church. Some conformists began to insist, for their part, that anyone who questioned the established order of the Church of England must be hell-bent on overthrowing it, perhaps even by force, and thus

---

5. The classic study of the rise of the Puritan movement, including the Admonition controversy, remains Patrick Collinson's *The Elizabethan Puritan Movement* (Berkeley: University of California Press, 1967).

might as well be traitors to the Crown. Into this tense controversy waded Richard Hooker.

Hooker's *Laws*

Hooker was by this time in his early thirties, having enjoyed academic success at Oxford and having just secured an enviable post as Master of the Temple Church in London—effectively the parish church for England's legal profession. With connections both to leading bishops like Edwin Sandys and to moderate Puritan leaders like John Rainolds, he was considered an ideal middle-of-the-road candidate. Unfortunately, his subordinate, the fiery presbyterian Walter Travers, lost little time in provoking a controversy with Hooker over his supposedly questionable teaching on justification and the status of the Roman Catholic Church. Hooker's ensuing sermons, later published as *A Learned Discourse on Justification*, represented one of the finest Reformation-era expositions of the doctrine and showcased his desire to find a middle path through controversy, using careful distinctions to distinguish the true contours of a doctrinal debate. These were skills he later put to use on a much larger scale in his *Laws of Ecclesiastical Polity*.

This work was occasioned by the rapid intensification of the Puritan controversy in the later 1580s. In particular, an anonymous Puritan pam-

phleteer calling himself "Martin Marprelate" published a series of scathing and scurrilous tracts de-
nouncing the bishops, which significantly raised the
rhetorical temperature of the controversy. The cap-
ture of a mentally unstable radical Puritan named
William Hacket, who claimed to be on a mission
from God to overthrow the Queen, made matters
far worse. The response from the authorities was to
tighten the screws, arresting several Puritan leaders and even executing a couple of the most radical
for treason, while leading churchmen poured forth
ponderous refutations of their arguments. Hooker,
who in 1591 moved to a quieter rural parish near
Canterbury, was determined to find a better way
forward through the conflict. *The Laws of Ecclesiastical Polity*, which he began sometime around 1590
and was still working on at his death in 1600, represented, according to C. S. Lewis, "a revolution in
the art of controversy."[6] Rather than engaging in
an increasingly exasperated blow-by-blow refutation, raining down hammer blows on the heads of
the opponents, Hooker sought to pull the rug out
from under their feet by going to the root of the
controversy. And while not above cutting sarcasm,
Hooker generally preferred a more conciliatory

---

6. C. S. Lewis, *English Literature in the Sixteenth Century, Excluding Drama*, vol. 3 of *The Oxford History of English Literature* (Oxford: Clarendon Press, 1954), 459.

tone, appealing to his opponents as men capable of rational persuasion.

He structured his *Laws* accordingly, beginning with a lengthy and masterful *Preface* that sought to clarify exactly what was at stake, warn of the dangers if radical principles were followed to their conclusion, and make a heartfelt appeal for reconciliation. What was at stake, then? To Hooker, basic principles of epistemology and authority. Many Puritans, in their haste to find fault with the (admittedly flawed) Elizabethan regime, had sought to stretch *sola Scriptura* beyond the breaking point, insisting that Scripture alone contained all the answers needed to resolve these controversies. Among the many dangers that Hooker spotted here, the worst was that it heightened the stakes enormously. No longer could Christian men of goodwill disagree over difficult prudential questions of church order; rather, it was to become a showdown of "those who took the Bible seriously" and those who did not. This also meant that there was no longer room to submit to God-given authorities in church and state with whom one disagreed. "We must obey God rather than men," insisted the more radical presbyterians, aligning themselves with the Apostles.

Hooker thus spent Book I of the *Laws* sketching out a grand vision of God's self-revelation first in his world and then in his Word, unfolding the many different orders of law that govern our lives and our relation to our fellow creatures and our Creator. This book is justly famous as a Protestant appropriation of the Aristotelian and Thomistic tradition of metaphysics and epistemology, and serves as a foundation for everything that follows. Book II turns to hermeneutics, asking if it is really true that Scripture intends to function as a comprehensive answer-book for human life. Book III then narrows the question to one of church order, clarifying the nature of the church, and distinguishing its unchangeable from its changeable features, so as to better discern how Scripture speaks (and often does not speak) to particular questions of church polity. In Book IV, he tackles another foundational principle of the Puritan case: that when in doubt, we should try to go as far from Rome as possible. For many Puritan leaders, if the Roman Catholic Church used a particular liturgical form or even term, that was good enough reason for the Church of England to reject it. Hooker instead offers a nuanced blueprint for how to critically appropriate traditional church practices: recognizing some as timeless treasures for the church, discarding some as mere superstition, and retrieving others from corruption to edification.

Purpose and Structure of Book V

Book IV, by showing that the liturgical practices of the Church of England are at least potentially defensible and edifying, sets the stage for Book V, which undertakes a thorough defense of them as edifying *in fact*. Readers of the *Laws*, after clambering their way through the difficult prose of Books I through IV (averaging around fifty pages in length), are often brought up short when they find themselves faced with the mammoth Book V, which clocks in at over 300 pages in most editions. No wonder that it took fully four years for it to appear after the first volume of the *Laws* (published in 1593). Why the imbalance? Research into the origins of Book V suggests that Hooker did not originally intend it to be nearly so long. On the contrary, sticking to his plan to avoid getting drawn into the weeds of controversy and to carry out the debate at the higher levels of principle, he initially penned a relatively short Book V that offered a positive exposition of the basic principles and elements of liturgical theology. Hooker scholar John Booty suggests that the original table of contents for Book V ran as follows:[7]

---

7. John E. Booty, ed., *The Folger Library Edition of the Works of Richard Hooker*, vol. 6.1, *Of the Lawes of Ecclesiasticall Politie, Commentary* (Binghamton: Medieval & Renaissance Texts and Studies, 1993), 189.

1–11: Introduction to a theology of worship, and the need to avoid the ditches of "atheism" and "superstition"

12 [18 in the final version]: A theology of preaching

13–15 [23–25]: A theology of prayer and the purpose of public prayer

16–22 [50–56]: Christ's incarnation and union with his people—the foundation of sacramental theology

23–25 [57–58, 67]: The sacraments in general, with a chapter each on baptism and the eucharist

26–27 [76–77]: The office of ordained ministry

Such a Book V would have been only around double the length of the earlier books, and would have marked a beautiful and timeless treatise of liturgical theology. However, evidence suggests that Hooker was heavily pressured by his friends and former pupils George Cranmer and Edwin Sandys to get deeper into the trenches with Puritan polemicists, offering a detailed response to their many particular criticisms of the Book of Common Prayer and English church practices. Accordingly, Hooker kept adding chapters, many of them addressing specific objections to the church's practice of public prayer (e.g., the recitation of the Lord's Prayer, Ch. 35), the sacraments (e.g., the use of godparents, Ch. 64), or ordination (e.g., ministeri-al vestments, Ch. 78). Other chapters touched on a range of other liturgical issues that do not fit neatly under any of these headings, such as his defense of the Athanasian Creed in Chapter 42 and of feast and fast days in chapters 69–72. Among the most beautiful and memorable chapters, probably added in the expanded version, is Chapter 38: "Of Music with Psalms." Notably, his section dealing with sac-ramental rites contains chapters on confirmation (Ch. 61) and matrimony (Ch. 73), although he does not consider these to be sacraments properly speaking.

The expanded Book V is a marvelous resource for any Anglican seeking to understand the mean-ing and practice of the Book of Common Prayer, as well as any historian investigating what typical English church practices looked like in the Eliza-bethan era. Many of the particular issues debated continue to be points of hot contention between Anglicans and Presbyterians today, or indeed be-tween more liturgically-minded and anti-liturgical wings within both communions. Readers may be surprised, for instance, to find that on issues such as the recitation of creeds or set prayers, or the cel-ebration of the church calendar, the terms of the debate have moved little from Hooker's day—al-though many of his arguments seem, at least to us, so compelling that you might think they would have settled the discussion long since.

However, it also cannot be denied that the expanded Book V is quite tedious at points, consumed sometimes with liturgical minutiae or largely obsolete practices like baptism by midwives and the churching of women. Accordingly, for the purposes of this modernization we elected not to simply plough through starting at Chapter 1 and ending at Chapter 81. Instead, in order to provide a readable resource of value to a very wide range of readers, and to whet the public appetite for more, we opted to begin first with the electrifying section on Christology and sacraments, widely renowned as the high point of the entire *Laws*. In these chapters Hooker first explains how God is in Christ Jesus through the hypostatic union, then how Christ is in his people by the mystical union, and finally how the sacraments serve as God's ordained means for initiating and strengthening this union. More than any other section of the *Laws*, these chapters represent something of a freestanding treatise in systematic theology that rises above the partisan conflict of the sixteenth century—although of course the latter can be frequently glimpsed in the background, as in references to the Lutheran doctrine of ubiquity and the doctrine of transubstantiation. The book before you then represents more or less Hooker's original "treatise on Christology

and sacraments," although with the additional in-
clusion of Chapters 59–60 (defending the necessity
of baptism as the ordinary—though not indispens-
able—means by which God brings about regeneration in believers) and Chapter 66 (defending the
usefulness of confirmation as marking the believer's
first entry into spiritual adulthood).

Although Hooker is frequently celebrated as
the great theologian of the Anglican Communion,
Protestants of other traditions—and indeed Roman
Catholics—should not be too quick to pass by on
the other side of the road. Much of the theology expressed in these chapters represents nothing more
or less than mere Christianity—a luminous and
sometimes lyrical exposition of the central mysteries of the Christian faith confessed in the early
councils and the ecumenical creeds. Even when he
gets to the disputed territory of sacramental theology, Hooker is extremely keen to "keep the main
thing the main thing," as it were, seeking to clear
the ground of distracting debates over secondary issues (such as the mode of Christ's eucharistic presence) and focus our attention on Christ himself, as
he truly offers himself to us in the sacrament. Of
course, there is no way to do this without taking
controversial stands *vis-à-vis* other Christian traditions, since when it comes to sacramental theology,
much of the disagreement concerns what *are* the
primary issues and which issues are secondary. So

it is that Hooker's valiant attempt to find the common ground between Reformed, Lutheran, and Roman Catholic eucharistic theologies in Chapter 67 can only go so far, and remains in the end a forthrightly Reformed formulation, albeit an unusually rich and irenic one.

Some readers may be surprised to hear Hooker described as "forthrightly Reformed," since Anglicans and "Reformed" today are liable to think of themselves in opposition to one another. But this certainly was not the case in the sixteenth or early seventeenth centuries, when there was no "Anglicanism," but simply the "English Reformed church," a national branch of a diverse international movement that included Swiss, French, Dutch, Scottish, German, and indeed Hungarian Reformed churches. The English were far from the only Reformed church in that day to practice a more elaborate liturgy than that typical of modern Presbyterians, although their retention of bishops was an unusual feature (but not one that overly troubled most of the continental Reformed). Still, it has been hard for modern readers—including many scholars—to shake the sense that there is something distinctively "Anglican" and thereby un-Reformed about Hooker's work, especially here in this crucial Book V. Indeed, the chapters appearing in this volume include two sections that have prompted frequent claims that Hooker is trying to steer the English church toward a more Lutheran and perhaps even more Catholic theology.

These readings, however, stem from largely from inattention toward the broader contours of sixteenth-century Reformed theology across Europe, which turns out to have been much more sacramental than most of its modern offspring.[8] It is to be hoped that a rediscovery of Richard Hooker will not only spur today's Anglican churches to reconnect with the riches of their heritage, but will also encourage a sacramental renewal among Presbyterians and other Reformed churches. Three points in particular warrant careful attention, although I will touch on them only briefly here in this introduction so that readers can hasten on to read Hooker's own exposition.

Key Doctrinal Themes

The Mystical Union

The chapters in this volume could be summed up as "Hooker's theology of participation." Yet this word, so important to the history of Christian theology, is a notoriously slippery one, and especially so in

---

8. As John Williamson Nevin demonstrated nearly two centuries ago. See John Williamson Nevin, *The Mystical Presence and the Doctrine of the Reformed Church on the Lord's Supper*, ed. Linden J. DeBie, vol. 1 of The Mercersburg Theology Study Series (Eugene: Wipf and Stock, 2012).

modern theology, where few words have become more pervasive. It is difficult to resist the sense that the newfound popularity of this theme owes much to its vagueness, the readiness with which it can be invoked to serve any number of purposes, tying together different theological topics, or creating the illusion of ecumenical convergence, without the hard work of distinction and definition. So it is that many readers of Hooker have tried to see in Book V a sub-Protestant blurring of the boundaries between Christ and us, in line with Roman Catholic or modern ecumenist theologies of the church as an "extension of the incarnation."

In fact, however, Hooker is very careful here, as elsewhere, to distinguish his terms. "The union or mutual inward hold which Christ has of us and we of him" (56.1) is simply not the same thing as the union or mutual inward hold of Christ's divine and human natures in the incarnation, although it is certainly made possible by it. We are not in God the same way that Jesus Christ was:

> God is not so in any creature, nor any creature so in God, as Christ—whether we consider him as the personal Word of God, or as the natural Son of man. All other things that are of God nonetheless do have God in them, and he has them in himself. Yet because their substance

and his wholly differ, their coherence and communion either with him or among themselves is in no way like that union between the persons discussed above (56.4–5).

Indeed, there are at least four sorts of union worth distinguishing: the union between the eternal persons of the Trinity; the union of the Word with Christ's human flesh; the union of the God-man with his people; and the union which all humans, saved and unsaved, have with God by virtue of creation: "All things have received from him their first being, and their continuance in being. All things are therefore partakers of God; they are his offspring; his influence is in them" (56.5). If we do not rightly distinguish between at least these four different unions or "participations," heresy lurks around every corner.[9]

To say this, of course, is not to minimize or spiritualize the profound union that does exist between the natural body of the incarnate Christ and the Church as his mystical body. Like Calvin, Hooker is keen to emphasize that, while hidden

---

9. For an excellent and comprehensive discussion of Hooker's theology of participation, see Paul Anthony Dominiak, *Richard Hooker: The Architecture of Participation* (London: T&T Clark, 2020).

and invisible, this union is not merely some spiritual connection of our souls with Christ's divine nature, as in much modern evangelical theology:

> Can anyone doubt that our own bodies receive from the flesh of Christ itself that life which shall make them glorious at the last day, and for which they are already accounted parts of his blessed body? Our corruptible bodies could never live the life they shall live were they not joined here with his incorruptible body....Christ is therefore, both as God and as man, that true vine of which we are both spiritually and corporeally branches (56.8).

These remarks about the mystical union serve as the ground of Hooker's sacramental theology, as he turns to consider the visible rituals that establish, nurture, and sustain this invisible union.

The Necessity of Sacraments

Here too, though, there has been ample confusion among many of Hooker's readers, who often hasten on from Chapter 56 (on the mystical union) to Chapter 58 (on the enactment of that union in baptism) without careful attention to Chapter 57, perhaps one of Hooker's most carefully-argued expositions in the *Laws*. Here he gives close attention to the all-important question of why and how it is that sacraments are necessary if, on a Protestant account, redemption is accomplished by grace alone through faith alone, by imputation of Christ's righteousness rather than by a medicinal infusion of it. Hooker is keen to avoid both a Socinian rationalism, in which sacraments have no purpose other than "*to teach* the mind—by other senses—what the Word teaches by hearing" (57.1), and a Roman Catholic *ex opere operato* theology, in which the sacraments accomplish the grace they signify automatically and almost mechanically.

Choosing his words extremely carefully, he writes that sacraments are "heavenly ceremonies, which God has sanctified and ordained to be administered in his church: first, as marks by which we know when God imparts the living or saving grace of Christ to all who are capable of receiving it; and second, as conditional means which God requires for those to whom he imparts grace" (57.3). Hooker's formulation here may be seen as an effort to forge a synthesis between what Brian Gerrish has called *symbolic parallelism*, in which the elements are symbols that signify that God is simultaneously but invisibly bestowing the grace of union with Christ upon worthy recipients, and *symbolic instrumentalism*, in which the elements actually serve somehow as the instruments through which

God bestows that grace upon worthy recipients.[10] (Hooker clearly rejects the doctrine, common among modern Protestants, that Gerrish designates as *symbolic memorialism*, in which the elements are symbols that serve as an occasion to publicly declare and remember the work of Christ.)

Thus we note that the first part of his definition clearly expresses parallelism: "marks by which we know when God imparts the living or saving grace of Christ to all who are capable of receiving it." Here, it is clearly *God* who does the imparting, and the sacraments serve simply as marks to tell us when. Hooker goes on to emphasize this in 57.4, rejecting any concept of an *ex opere operato* efficacy to sacraments: "they are not necessary to supernatural life in just the same way that food is to natural life, because they do not contain *in themselves* any vital power or efficacy." Thus it is that not all who receive the elements receive the grace—the grace is only for those who are "capable of receiving it." Hooker, however, is willing to go beyond parallelism and speak of an instrumentalism, if carefully defined. Hence the second part of his definition, that sacraments are "conditional means which God requires for those to whom he imparts grace." In

---

10. Brian A. Gerrish, *Grace and Gratitude: The Eucharistic Theology of John Calvin* (Minneapolis: Fortress Press, 1993), 167.

other words, not merely does God freely bestow grace alongside the sacraments, but he has so ordered the economy of redemption that the grace thereby bestowed is made contingent on our faithful reception of them: "it is not *ordinarily* his will to bestow the grace of the sacraments on anyone except by the sacraments" (57.4, emphasis Hooker's). From this standpoint, they may be spoken of as instruments, not because there is anything in the sacraments themselves that makes them effectual in this regard, but simply because God has chosen to designate them as prerequisites, as it were, for pouring out his grace.

This is what he means by calling them "*moral* instruments of salvation": they are "duties of service and worship, which are unprofitable unless we perform them as the author of grace requires" (57.4). I may promise my son that if he cheerfully performs his regular chores, he will enjoy the blessing of quality time reading with me; by this, I make the chores to be a "moral instrument" of receiving the promised grace. The metaphor is of course inadequate in that the quality time is temporally separated from the chore, whereas the union enjoyed by means of the sacraments is ordinarily simultaneous. But it highlights the essentials of what Hooker wishes to convey: (1) the grace is not internal to the physical action, but conditioned upon it; (2) the physical action is not enough, but must be accompanied by an attitude of faith and gratitude; (3) the promise is nonetheless sure: God will not fail to bestow the grace; (4) the grace is genuinely *gracious*; it is not *owed* to us. Hooker's own example is that of the bronze serpent: the Israelites had to turn to it in faith to be healed, but "he who turned toward it was saved, not by what he saw, but by thee, the Savior of all."

This careful formulation establishes the basis upon which Hooker is willing to use the language of "instruments" or "causes" of grace in relation to the sacraments, and it is unfortunate that so many readers of Hooker have read the expositions on baptism and the eucharist without first digesting the definitions he lays down in V.57. These definitions enable Hooker to consistently make three points throughout his exposition of baptism and the eucharist: (1) to be sure, God *can*, and in extraordinary cases *does*, give sacramental grace without the administration and reception of the sacraments; (2) however, given his clear commands to us to observe the sacraments, we have no business testing him, but must make it our first priority to receive (and, in the case of clergy, to administer) the sacraments; (3) since the sacraments are not "physical instruments," we must receive them with faith in order to enjoy the promised benefits.

What then are these promised benefits? We know already from V.56 that they must pertain to the mystical life-giving union with the incarnate Christ, so vividly described there. But is there any difference between baptism and the eucharist? Yes. "We receive Christ Jesus in baptism once as the first beginner of our life, and in the eucharist repeatedly to bring our life by degrees to its completion" (57.6). Having cautioned clearly against putting too much stock in the elements themselves, Hooker feels free to speak in very strong terms of what God intends to accomplish by means of our reception of them. Regarding baptism, Hooker elaborates that by it we are "incorporated into Christ" and thus "obtain that saving grace of imputation, which takes away all former guilt through his most precious merit, as well as that infused divine virtue of the Holy Ghost that gives the powers of the soul their first disposition towards future newness of life" (60.2), and that it is "the door of our actual entrance into God's house, the first apparent beginning of life—perhaps a seal to the grace of election previously received, but the first step to our sanctification here on earth" (60.3).[11] Regarding the

---

11. Hooker does not, alas, explain how to reconcile this saving grace given to all who are baptized with the fact that clearly not all the baptized are saved in the end. Clearly for Hooker, apostasy from a state of initial justification is a real possibility, even if the elect will surely persevere to the end. The thorny questions regarding the relationship of sacramental grace, election, and apostasy that were to trouble the Re-

eucharist, Hooker elaborates, "those who have laid the foundation and reached the first beginning of new life in baptism find here in the Eucharist the nourishment and food that ensures the continuation of this life in them. Those who desire to live the life of God must eat the flesh and drink the blood of the Son of Man, for without this diet, we cannot live" (67.1).

Eucharistic Ecumenism?

Hooker's exposition of the eucharist in Chapter 67 of Book V is justly accounted as one of the greatest sections of the *Laws*, or perhaps of all English theological literature. It also represents a moving call, at the end of a century of bitter controversy which had divided not only Protestants from Catholics, but from one another, to "Let disputes and questions—the enemies of piety and hindrances to true devotion, which on this matter have been too patiently heard—take their rest" (67.12). But its beauty and irenicism have sometimes also conspired to obscure some of the clear theological lines being drawn here.

---

formed in the seventeenth century had not yet been pressed as forcefully as they would soon be, and although Hooker's *Dublin Fragments* might have given us a fuller exposition on the issue, they never came close to completion before his untimely death.

To be sure, Hooker is indeed very eager to forge a pathway to peace when it comes to the all-important eucharistic question. As large as the issues of justification by faith or *sola Scriptura* loom in hindsight when we consider the battle-lines of the Reformation, we can often forget that if Protestants were burned at the stake, it was usually because of their refusal to affirm transubstantiation. And the early rift between Lutheran and Reformed wings of the Reformation, crystallized by the Formula of Concord in 1577, stemmed above all from rival understandings (or misunderstandings of one another's understandings) of Christ's eucharistic presence. Hooker thus frames his chapter on the eucharist, penned toward the very end of the tumultuous sixteenth century, as a call to put aside all such bitterness and get back to the point of the sacrament.

Accordingly, Hooker begins his account by trying to highlight what nearly all the warring doctrines have in common. He takes for granted that all parties in his day are agreed in rejecting the mere memorialist doctrine,[12] in which the sacrament is "a shadow, destitute, empty, and void of Christ." The

---

12. An intriguing remark, given that much secondary literature today continues to mistakenly claim that Zwinglian memorialism was a dominant doctrine in the Elizabethan Church, especially among Puritans.

Reformed then (whether Bullingerian or Calvinistic), the Lutheran, and indeed the Catholics are all agreed in affirming a "*real participation* in Christ and in the life of his body and blood *by means of this sacrament*," so why "should the world continue to be distracted and torn apart by so many fights, when the only remaining controversy is *where* Christ is?" Indeed, all parties agree that "the *soul of man* is the receptacle of Christ's presence" (67.2, emphasis Hooker's), so that the disagreement only concerns whether the presence is *only* there (as the Reformed say) or also somehow in the bread and wine (as the Lutherans and Catholics say in their own distinctive ways). Hooker laments this as a foolish debate: "I should wish that men would spend more time meditating with silence on *what* we have by the sacrament, and less on disputing about *how*....Curious and intricate speculations hinder, abate, and quench those inflamed motions of delight and joy which divine graces raise when extraordinarily present to us" (67.3).

However, Hooker's call to peace is certainly not the anti-intellectual's throwing up of the hands and saying, "Oh, who cares about these abstract speculations? Let's just agree to disagree!" Hooker takes some time to explain why it is that the Reformed doctrine conveys all that Scripture and patristic reason require, and makes clear that he deems both Lutheran consubstantiation and Catholic transubstantiation to be confusing, baseless, and contrary to reason. To be sure, he does not exactly object to people believing these doctrines so much as to insisting on the necessity of others believing them; while he thinks both doctrines wrong-headed, his main point is that they are simply *unnecessary*. Thus he asks,

> Why then do we vainly trouble ourselves with such fierce contentions about consubstantiation and transubstantiation, and whether or not the sacrament itself first possesses Christ or not? Whatever the answer might be, it can neither help or hinder us…. Take what we all agree on, and then consider whether we should not leave the remaining questions to one side as superfluous, rather than insisting on them as necessary (67.6–7).

But we should note that this is itself a controversial claim, however much Hooker wishes it were not, for both Roman Catholics (at Trent) and Lutherans (in the Formula of Concord) were on record as indeed insisting upon their claims about Christ's bodily presence *in the consecrated elements* as indeed necessary. Thus, while Hooker is proposing the Reformed doctrine of the eucharist as a kind of ecumenical meeting-ground on which he hopes conflicts may be laid to rest, we must not lose sight of the fact that he is indeed proposing *the Reformed doctrine of the eucharist* as this meeting-ground; there is indeed strictly speaking no neutral third ground between those who say that a doctrine is necessary and those who say it is not.

This controversial stance in Chapter 67, of course, rests upon an earlier set of positions that Hooker states out in Chapters 54–55. All the eucharistic controversies of the sixteenth century quickly led back to Christology, with the various disputing parties seeking to map their positions onto the coordinates established by the fifth-century Councils of Chalcedon and Ephesus. Thus it is that Hooker prefaces his discussions of sacraments with the luminous exposition of Chalcedonian Christology that occupies the first few chapters of this volume. Less historically-attuned readers, however, may miss the significance of the lengthy discussion of "the personal presence of Christ everywhere" in Chapter 55. This had been a subject of fierce debate both among Lutheran theologians, and between Lutheran and Reformed theologians beginning in the 1550 and continuing through at least the 1580s. Many Lutherans, following Wurttemberg theologian Johannes Brenz, had contended that the eucharistic presence of Christ was made possible by the "ubiquity" of his human body, which was supposed to have received the properties of divinity by virtue of the hypostatic union. The Reformed argued that this represented a violation of the Chalcedonian Definition's insistence that there was no "mixture" or "confusion" of the two natures, and that although Christ's humanity could be said to be present in some sense wherever his divinity was, this sense must be carefully circumscribed to avoid Christological heresy. Although Hooker has sometimes been misunderstood or misrepresented on this point, a careful reading of Chapters 54–55 in the context of sixteenth-century debates shows him siding resolutely with the Reformed position, although he seeks to frame it as irenically as possible.[13]

Finally, there is no point in obscuring the fact that Hooker's eucharistic theology is unambiguously receptionist. That is to say, in keeping with his general remarks about the sacraments as "moral instruments," he seeks to stress that there is no gracious change, nor presence of Christ, in the elements as such, but only in the faithful receiver. This would seem so clear as to be unworthy of comment except for the fact that a striking number of Hooker scholars (influenced often by an Anglo-Cathol-

---

13. For a full discussion, see Brad Littlejohn, "A Reformed Irenic Christology: Richard Hooker and the Question of Ubiquity in the 16th Century," in Brad Littlejohn, ed., *Beyond Calvin: Essays on the Breadth of the Reformed Tradition* (Landrum, SC: The Davenant Press, 2017): 63–106.

icism that seeks to align English liturgical practice more closely with the medieval era) have sought to claim otherwise. A few passages will suffice: "the real presence of Christ's most blessed body and blood should not be looked for in the sacrament, but in the worthy receiver of the sacrament." "I do not see any way to gather from Christ's words when and where the bread becomes his body or the cup his blood, except within the heart and soul of the one who receives them. The sacraments really *exhibit*, but from what we can gather from the text *are* not really, nor do they really *contain* in themselves, that grace which it pleases God to bestow with them or by them." "There is no sentence in Holy Scripture that says we cannot be made partakers of his body and blood by this sacrament unless the sacrament itself first contains or is converted into them" (all from 67.6).

Chapter 67, then, paradoxically represents both an attempt to forge a pathway of peace through the midst of seemingly interminable doctrinal controversy, and at the same time a forthright statement of one side of that controversy—namely, the Reformed view. In this, it is representative of much of the *Laws*, which is notable not so much for offering a uniquely Anglican theological synthesis, but rather for offering a distinctive theological tone or posture: one which takes doctrine extremely seriously, but also goes out of its way to understand opposing viewpoints and demonstrate the wide extent of common ground, and which refuses to major on the minors. May such a posture of Reformational irenicism re-animate our churches today.

Editorial Approach

Modernizing Hooker's prose was a complex task, certainly more complicated than updating a few archaic words and breaking apart a few lengthy sentences. Hooker's sentences are not just lengthy; his syntax itself is often dense and unwieldy, even by sixteenth century standards, and so the majority of sentences required syntactical reworking of some kind. Hooker's idioms and turns of phrase are also frequently archaic or rhetorically elevated in Shakespearean ways that can be obscure to the modern reader, so our vocabulary updates were extensive. Our project is therefore a deep and pervasive one, with the outcome being more akin to a *translation* than a modernization.

In general, our method was as follows. Patrick Timmis would separately read and carefully rewrite Hooker's prose, translating Hooker's meaning and prose into modern parlance. This first pass was fairly conservative; Patrick focused on breaking Hooker's towering and often syntactically obscure sentences into more manageable lengths, updating archaic vocabulary and syntax, and identifying passages that were particularly ambiguous or difficult for further discussion. Brad Littlejohn then did a second pass, comparing Hooker's original to the draft translation and sometimes moving that translation in a more contemporary direction to fit the style of the earlier volumes. Where necessary, Brad suggested solutions to interpretive ambiguities with reference to clearer portions of Hooker's works. He then sent this second draft back to Patrick for review. In this way we worked through Hooker's work, sentence by sentence, paragraph by paragraph, with an eye towards style, subtle connotations in the text, and key terms in Hooker's argument. It was a laborious process, and often the final version would end up looking markedly different than the first draft. Brian Marr then took the final version, replaced Hooker's translations of patristic texts with contemporary scholarly translations (most often from Philip Schaff's *Nicene and Post-Nicene Fathers* or New City Press's Augustine series), and regularized the citations. Finally, we read through the entire modernized version on its own, with this final round of edits focused on hearing and remedying any needless impediments to clarity or readability.

Since our goal in this "translation" process was to render Hooker's prose easily accessible to a modern audience, we adopted a method that in traditional terms would be considered dynamic rather than literal. The goal was to convey Hooker's *meaning* as accurately and intuitively as possible to a modern audience. We felt free to use reasonably modern colloquialisms, though we also eschewed any words or phrases that smacked entirely of the current century. We often found that such phrases, transparently modern as they were, drew attention to themselves rather than to the underlying text. This defeated one of our main goals, which was to remove as many distractions as possible from the meaning that Hooker was trying to convey, allowing it to shine through without occasioning the reader any uncomfortable pauses. Indeed, when in doubt, we erred in favor of what might be a more nineteenth- than twenty-first-century English style, when the latter was so clearly incongruous with the subject matter as to feel out of place. For this reason, there were certain conventions that we did not seek to bring into line with common twenty-first-century standards, most notable among them Hooker's convention of using masculine nouns and pronouns where gender-neutral ones are now widely preferred. To change his "man" to "humanity" or his "he" to "he or she" would have been so incongruous with the habits of his age as to have drawn needless attention to itself.

For devotees of Hooker's original, let it not be thought that we needlessly flattened out his often noble rhetoric and remarkable turns of phrase into a bland, flat, and simplistic sentence structure. On the contrary, if the basic phrasing and rhetorical cadence of the original could be retained without great loss of comprehensibility, we did our utmost to preserve it. Some famous and luminous passages we left virtually untouched. Any reader of Hooker cannot but come away with an enhanced ear for the English language, for words that sound crisp or sonorous and those that are flat and dull. Thus, even when it was clear to us that we would have to find some more modern synonym for a now-obsolete term, we often puzzled long over a single word until we found the one that did the job without detracting from the elegance of the original.

Recognizing that Hooker's chapter titles are frequently lengthy and ponderous, as was conventional for the sixteenth century, we decided for this volume to include pithier, more modern-sounding chapter titles of our own devising. Beneath each of these, a modernized adaptation of Hooker's original appears as a subtitle of sorts.

Examples of Changes

Below are a few examples to give a sense of cases when extensive reworking was sometimes necessary, of when a few judicious changes did the trick, and of when almost no change at all was called for.

Here is a short passage where complexity of syntax, archaism of language, and indeed archaism of thought all conspire to render comprehension quite difficult for the contemporary reader, and required some filling-in-the-blanks to make sense of Hooker's meaning:

> There are that elevate too much the ordinary
> and immediate means of life, relying
> wholly
> upon the bare conceit of that eternal election,
> which notwithstanding includeth a
> subordination of means without which we
> are not actually brought to enjoy what
> God secretly
> did intend; and therefore to build upon
> God's election if we keep not ourselves to
> the ways
> which he hath appointed for men to walk in,
> is but a self-deceiving vanity
> (*Original*, 60.3).

There are some people who focus almost exclusively on the bare notion of their own eternal election as the ordinary and immediate means of grace. But predestination includes a subordination of means, without which we are not actually brought to enjoy what God has secretly intended for us. It is a self-deceiving vanity, then, to rest upon God's election if we do not ourselves keep to the ways which he has appointed for men to walk in (*Our version*, 60.3).

Below is a paragraph where our interventions were more restrained, and primarily focused on making Hooker's long and complex sentences more structurally manageable (typically by breaking particularly complex sentences into shorter, simpler ones):

Wherefore a necessity there is of receiving, and a necessity of administering, the sacrament of baptism; the one peradventure not so absolute as some have thought, but out of all peradventure the other more strait and narrow, than that the church which is by office a mother unto such as crave at her hands the sacred mystery of their new birth, should repel them and see them die unsatisfied of these their ghostly desires, rather than give them their soul's rights with omission of those things that serve but only for the more convenient and orderly administration thereof. For as on the one side we grant that those sentences of Holy Scripture which make sacraments most necessary to eternal life are no prejudice to their salvation that want them by some inevitable necessity, and without any fault of their own; so it ought in reason to be likewise acknowledged, that forasmuch as our Lord himself maketh baptism necessary, necessary whether we respect the good received by baptism, or the testimony thereby yielded unto God of that humility and meek obedience, which reposing wholly itself on the absolute authority of his commandment, and on the truth of his heavenly promise, doubteth not but from creatures despicable in their own condition and substance to obtain grace of inestimable value, or rather not from them but from him, yet by them as by his appointed means; howsoever he by the secret ways of his own incomprehensible mercy may be thought to save without baptism, this cleareth not the Church from guiltiness of blood, if through her superfluous scrupulosity lets and impediments of less regard should cause a grace of so great moment to be withheld, wherein our merciless strictness may be our own harm, though not theirs towards whom we shew it; and we for the hardness of our hearts may perish, albeit they through God's unspeakable mercy do live (*Original*, 60.7).

There is, then, a necessity of receiving and a necessity of administering the sacrament of baptism. The first is perhaps not so absolute as some have thought, but the second is if anything more rigid. Should the church, called to be a mother to those who crave at her hands the sacred mystery of their new birth, repel them and see them die with their spiritual desires unsatisfied, rather than give them their souls' rights, even if it means omitting those things that serve only for more convenient and orderly administration? Consider: we grant on the one side that those statements of Holy Scripture which make sacraments most necessary to eternal life do not threaten the salvation of those who lack them because of some inevitable necessity and through no fault of their own. But we must on the other side reasonably acknowledge that our Lord himself makes baptism necessary—both as regards the good received from baptism and the testimony of humility and meek obedience that we show to God by receiving it. Reposing entirely on the absolute authority of his commandment and on the truth of his heavenly promise, our obedience does not doubt that it will obtain grace of inestimable value even from such lowly creatures—or rather, receive grace from God, but through these creatures as his appointed means. However it may be that God saves without baptism through the secret ways of his own incomprehensible mercy, the church is not cleared from bloodguilt if through her superfluous scrupulosity she withholds the momentous grace of baptism on account of trivial impediments. Such merciless strictness may greatly harm us, if not those to whom we show it. We may perish for the hardness of our hearts, though they live through God's unspeakable mercy (*Our version*, 60.7).

On the other hand, there were plenty of cases where Hooker's prose was so crisp or pithy, or so elegant and luminous, that to undertake more than very minor changes would be needless and harmful. The peroration to the climactic chapter on the eucharist, for instance, is such a wonderful opportunity to hear Hooker preach that we have left it virtually untouched:

> Let it therefore be sufficient for me presenting myself at the Lord's table to know what there I receive from him, without searching or inquiring of the manner how Christ performeth his promise; let disputes and questions, enemies to piety, abatements of true devotion, and hitherto in this cause but over patiently heard, let them take their rest; let curious and sharpwitted men beat their heads about what questions themselves will, the very letter of the word of Christ giveth plain security that these mysteries do as nails fasten us to his very Cross, that by them we draw out, as touching efficacy, force, and virtue, even the blood of his gored side, in the wounds of our Redeemer we there dip our tongues, we are dyed red both within and without, our hunger is satisfied and our thirst for ever quenched;

they are things wonderful which he
feeleth, great which he seeth and unheard
of which he uttereth, whose soul is possessed of this Paschal Lamb and made joy-
ful in the strength of this new wine, this
bread hath in it more than the substance
which our eyes behold, this cup hallowed
with solemn benediction availeth to the
endless life and welfare both of soul and
body, in that it serveth as well for a medicine to heal our infirmities and purge our
sins as for a sacrifice of thanksgiving; with
touching it sanctifieth, it enlighteneth
with belief, it truly conformeth us unto
the image of Jesus Christ; what these elements are in themselves it skilleth not,
it is enough that to me which take them
they are the body and blood of Christ, his
promise in witness hereof sufficeth, his
word he knoweth which way to accomplish; why should any cogitation possess
the mind of a faithful communicant but
this, O my God thou art true, O my Soul
thou art happy! (*Original*, 67.11).

Let it be enough for me, then, when I
present myself at the Lord's table, to know
what I receive from him there, without searching or inquiring *how* Christ

performs his promise. Let disputes and questions—the enemies of piety and hindrances to true devotion, which on this matter have been too patiently heard—take their rest. Let curious and sharp-witted men beat their heads about what questions they like. The very letter of the word of Christ gives plain assurance that these mysteries fasten us as nails to his very cross, that by them we draw out even the efficacy, power, and virtue of the blood from his gored side, that we there dip our tongues in the wounds of our Redeemer and are dyed red both within and without, that our hunger is satisfied and our thirst forever quenched. He whose soul possesses this paschal lamb and rejoices in the strength of this new wine feels wonderful things, sees great things, and utters unheard-of things. This bread contains more than the substance which our eyes behold. This cup, hallowed with a solemn benediction, avails to the endless life and health of both soul and body, for it serves both as a medicine to heal our infirmities and purge our sins, and as a sacrifice of thanksgiving. It sanctifies what it touches, enlightens us with belief, and truly conforms us to the image of Jesus Christ. It matters not what these elements are in themselves; it is enough that to me who receive them they are the body and blood of Christ. His promise suffices as a witness of this; he knows how to accomplish his words. Why should any thought possess the mind of the faithful communicant but this: "Oh my God, you are true. O my soul, you are happy"? (*Our version*, 67.12).

Textual Notes

The foundation text for Hooker's *Laws* is widely available, and a free copy is available online at the "Online Library of Liberty" (URL as of January 30, 2024: https://oll.libertyfund.org/title/keble-the-works-of-richard-hooker-vol-2). This represents a digitization of the seventh edition of Keble's 1832 edition of Hooker's *Works*, revised by the Very Rev. R. W. Church and the Rev. F. Paget in three volumes (Oxford: Clarendon Press, 1888).

The section numbers noted in parentheses reflect the "paragraph" numbers provided by John Keble in his 1832 edition, which have been adopted as standard in all subsequent editions of Hooker's work. You will note that we also sometimes included additional paragraph breaks within these numbered sections, here too following the precedent established by the edition on the Online Library of Liberty, as we found that more frequent paragraph breaks improved readability. We found it most helpful to retrieve citations from A. S. McGrade's new Oxford University Press edition (*Of the Laws of Ecclesiastical Polity: A Critical Edition with Modern Spelling*), and are very grateful to Prof. McGrade for his labors in providing full citations whenever possible from Hooker's original cryptic notes.

Please note that double quotation marks do not necessarily imply verbatim quotations; Cartwright and other sixteenth-century English quotations are quite challenging, so they are modernized like Hooker. In a few cases where Hooker quoted loosely from Scripture or an ancient source, or used his own idiosyncratic translation, we chose to follow (and as necessary, modernize) his version rather than quoting from a standard modern translation, which we provided instead in a footnote. However, our general rule, for quotations of non-English texts, was to use a standard modern translation and reference it accordingly. Likewise, all Scripture quotations are from the NKJV, and all Apocryphal quotations from the Revised Standard Version, unless otherwise noted.

Note also that, in this installment of the *Laws*, we have shifted from placing scriptural citations in footnotes to including them in square brackets within the body of the text. This is to bring this volume more in line with other LEEP books published since our last Hooker work in 2019, reflecting changing and improving Davenant Press editorial standards. The vast majority of citations are original to Hooker, and were originally in footnote or margins. Where citations have been added by the editors to aid the reader, they are preceded "*Ed.*"

Further to this, readers will notice two sets of chapter numbers—one set in Roman numerals at the top of each chapter, and then one in Arabic numerals within the chapter title. The Roman numerals number the chapters by their ordering in this particular volume. The Arabic numerals give the chapter numbers within Book V as a whole. Since this volume picks up at Book V, Chapter 50, we wanted to minimize any reader confusion, but still make this volume's relation to the whole of the *Laws* clear, as well as provide a consistent system of reference. The original chapter numbers, given in Arabic numerals, are used for any references.

We have tried to be very sparse in making any editorial interjections beyond what is strictly necessary, but you will find a few places where we found an explanatory note in order, without which Hooker's meaning was likely to remain opaque to most readers.

CHAPTER I

50. What Are Sacraments?

On the sacraments: their names, their author, and their power. Their power is that God has ordained the sacraments as means to make us partakers of him in Christ, and of life through Christ.

(1.) Teaching and prayer, which we have previously discussed, are the building blocks of all other Christian duties. The most important of these are the sacraments of the church. The church is the mother of our new birth, in whose womb we are conceived, and at whose breasts we are nourished. All who (so far as we can tell) are born of God had the seed of their regeneration planted by the church's ministry, which uses for this purpose not only the Word, but also the sacraments, both of which have generative power and virtue.

(2.) The Church Fathers commonly used the name "sacraments" to refer to any articles of faith or religious duties which depend, not on common sense or natural reason, but on Christian revelation. More properly speaking, when we say "sacrament" we mean one of the primary divine ceremonies which include two things: visible actions or elements, and beyond that some hidden reality in reference to which we discern that rite to be a sacrament. We revere the holy sacraments, not by focusing on the service we give to God in celebrating them, but on the dignity of the sacred and secret gift God gives to us in receiving them. If only God can give to ceremonies the supernatural grace that makes them sacraments, how should any but God's church administer these rites, since none but God's church can recognize them as sacraments?

(3.) When it comes to sacraments, we must pay attention both to their power and to the proper form of their administration. Since sacraments are only necessary if they are effectual, we cannot discern why and how we need them until we see their effects. When sacraments are said to be 'visible signs of invisible grace,' we conceive that grace truly is the purpose for which these heavenly mysteries were instituted.[1] The material substance of a sac-

---

1. This phrase is often attributed to Augustine, though it does

rament signifies, figures, and represents this grace. But we will not truly understand the sacraments' efficacy unless we specify which grace in particular they point to, and how precisely they work in relation to that grace.

(4.) We only use sacraments in this life. But because they concern a far better life, they are accompanied by the grace which works salvation. Sacraments are the powerful instruments of God to eternal life. Our natural life consists in the union of our body with our soul; our supernatural life in the union of our soul with God. Because there can be no union between God and man without a mediator who is both, we should first consider how God is in Christ. Then we must turn to how Christ is in us, and how the sacraments serve to make us partakers of Christ. (The weightiness of this topic will not allow us to be brief on these points.)

---

not appear in this exact articulation anywhere in his work. However, it has come to be a shorthand summary of the sacramental theology of Augustine and all those who see themselves as standing in continuity with him.

51. The Divinity of the Incarnate Son

That God is in Christ by the personal incarnation of the Son, who is very God.

(1.) "The Lord our God is but one God" [*Ed.* Deut. 6:4]. While God is an indivisible unity, we adore the Father as existing altogether of himself, we glorify that consubstantial Word who is the Son, and we bless and magnify that co-essential Spirit eternally proceeding from both who is the Holy Ghost. Seeing therefore that the Father is of none, the Son is of the Father, and the Spirit is of both, they are by these properties really distinguishable from one another. For God's substance with the property *to be of none* defines the person of the Father; the very same one substance with the property *to be of the Father* defines the person of the Son; the same substance plus the property of *proceeding from the other two* defines the person of the Holy Ghost. So in each person is implied both the one substance of God and also that property which causes each person really and truly to differ from the other two. Every person has his own *subsistence* which no one else has, although there are others who share the same *substance*. No man but Peter can be Peter, but Paul has the exact same nature which Peter has. Again, all angels have the nature of pure and invisible spirits, but not all angels are the angel who appeared in a dream to Joseph.

(2.) Now when God became man, so that we should not err in assigning this humanity to the person of the Father or of the Spirit, St. Peter confessed to Christ that "Thou art *the Son* of the Living God" [*Ed*. Mt. 16:16] and St. John's exposition of the event was plain: it is *the Word* which was made Flesh [*Ed*. Jn. 1:14]. "The Father and the Holy Spirit," John of Damascus says, "Take no part at all in the incarnation of the Word except…in respect of good will and purpose."[1] Nevertheless, because the

----

1. John of Damascus, *Exposition of the Orthodox Faith* 3.11, trans. James L. Salmond, in *A Select Library of the Nicene and Post-Nicene Fathers*, Second Series, vol. 9, *St. Hilary of*

Word and deity are one subject, we must beware of excluding the nature of God from the incarnation, and of thus making the incarnate Son of God *not* very God. Without a doubt, God's very nature is incarnate in the only person of the Son, and has taken flesh to itself. So incarnation must neither be assigned to any person but the one, nor denied to that nature which is common to all three.

(3.) What is the cause of this incomprehensible mystery? It seems incongruous that the world should honor anyone as the Savior but him whom it honors as the Creator of the world, and in his wisdom God has not thought it appropriate to admit any way of saving man but by man himself. From these we may perceive a sufficient cause for why the divine nature should assume the human—that God might thus, in Christ, be reconciling the world to himself [*Ed.* 2 Cor. 5:19]. This is to say nothing of God's love and mercy towards man, which in the incarnation became a spectacle that neither men nor angels can behold without a kind of heavenly astonishment. But why, we may ask, should it be the Son, rather than either the Father or the Holy Ghost, who should be made man for this end and purpose? Consider: how could we, who are born

---

Poitiers, John of Damascus, ed. Philip Schaff and Henry Wace (New York: Charles Scribner's Sons, 1899), 55.

the children of wrath, be adopted as the sons of God through grace, by any other way than the natural Son of God becoming the Mediator between God and us? It was fitting, therefore, for him by whom all things exist to be the way of salvation for all, so that both the institution and the restitution of the world might both be wrought by one hand. The world's salvation was impossible without the incarnation of the Son of God—not impossible in and of itself, but impossible presupposing that the will of God was to have it saved no other way than by the death of his own Son. Therefore, having taken to himself our flesh, and by his incarnation making it his own flesh, the Son now had from us as his very own that which he should offer to God for us. Christ then took manhood so that by it he might be capable of the death to which he humbled himself. By that manhood he feels compassion and profound pity, which make the scepter of his dominion over the kingdom of heaven sweet and gracious. Thus he who could not suffer on earth for the sins of the world without our nature, now by means of that nature both makes intercession to God for sinners and exercises dominion over all men with a true, natural, and deeply-felt touch of mercy.

CHAPTER III

52. Christological Heresies

Heretical misinterpretations of the manner in which God and man are united in one Christ.

(1.) It is beyond man's ability either to perfectly express or even to understand the manner in which this was brought to pass. But the strength of our faith is tested by those things in which our wits are too weak. Because this divine mystery is more true than it is clear, many who have explained it according to their own ideas and imaginings turn out to offer expositions more clear than they are true. Indeed, for five hundred years after Christ, the church was almost wholly occupied in defending this article of faith from the sinister misconstructions of heretics.

(2.) The first mists of these heresies were dispelled by the light of the Council of Nicea.1 But it was not long before Macedonius transferred to God's Holy Spirit the same blasphemy by which Arius had already dishonored his co-eternally begotten Son, and not long before Apollinarius began to whittle away at Christ's humanity. After the Church Fathers Athanasius, Basil, and the two Gregories had by their strenuous efforts sufficiently refuted these impieties and vindicated the truth—no less for the deity of the Holy Ghost than for the complete humanity of Christ—there finally came a conclusive settlement. First a smaller and more intimate synod at Rome, and then the famous general council at Constantinople, brought all these controversies (and those which Paul of Samosata, Sabellius, Photinus, Aëtius, Eunomius, and the whole swarm of pestilent Demi-Arians had been stirring up periodically since the Council of Nicea) to a peaceful and quiet end.2 One hundred and fifty bishops there agreed upon a confession which remains a part of our church liturgy at this present hour, as a memorial to their fidelity and zeal, and a supreme safeguard for God's people against the venomous infection of heresy.

---

1. First Council of Nicaea, held in 325 AD.

2. First Council of Constantinople, held in 381 AD.

(3.) Thus the doctrine that Christ unites the fullness of God and the complete substance of man was established with full agreement throughout the world, till such a time as the heresy of Nestorius reared its head: "dividing Christ into two persons, the Son of God and the Son of man; the former a person begotten of God before all worlds, the latter another person born of the Virgin Mary, specially favored and chosen to be joined with the Son of God above all men, so that whoever desires to honor God must also honor Christ, with whose person God has deigned to join himself in such a high degree of gracious respect and favor."3 But Nestorius would never admit that the very same person who is truly man is also properly God—and that not by two persons being linked in love, but by two natures (human and divine) joined in one and the same person. Thus he could not admit that we may just as properly say that the God of glory suffered death as that he raised the dead from their graves, and that the Son of Man made the world as well as redeemed it.

What deceived Nestorius was his lack of attention to the very beginning of that wondrous union of God with man. "The Word (says St. John) be-

---

3. Hooker seems to be loosely paraphrasing and synthesizing passages from Cyril of Alexandria's *Epistle to Eulogius* 44 and Leontius's *On Sects*.

came flesh and dwelt *in us*" [Jn. 1:14].4 The Evangelist uses the grammatical plural—"men" when he speaks of manhood, "*us*" to refer to our human nature—just as the Apostle, when he denies Christ's assumption of *angelical nature*, also uses the plural: "He took not *Angels* but the seed of Abraham" [Heb. 2:16].5 It did not please the Word or Wisdom of God to take to itself some one person among men; for then that one who was divinely assumed would have been elevated, but no others. But Wisdom, in order that she might save many, built her house out of that *nature* which is common to all. She did not make *this or that man* her habitation, but dwelt *in us*. Before they take root and grow, seeds are only herbs or plants in possibility, not yet in actuality. If the Son of God had taken to himself a man already created and fully formed, it would necessarily follow that in Christ are two persons: the one assuming and the other assumed. In fact, the Son of God did not assume a man's person unto his own, but a man's nature to his own person. He therefore took *semen*, the seed of Abraham, the very first original element of our nature, before it had come to have

4. We follow Hooker's rendering here rather than regularizing the text to the NKJV. All ensuing biblical quotations will come from the NKJV, unless otherwise noted.

5. Hooker is drawing on Hebrews 2:16 here, though not directly quoting the scriptural text.

any personal human subsistence. The flesh, and the conjunction of that flesh with God, both began at the same instant. God's making and taking to himself our flesh was only one act, so that in Christ there is only one personal subsistence, and that one is from everlasting. By taking only the nature of man, Christ still continues as the same person, and changes only the manner of his subsisting, which was before solely in the glory of the Son of God, but is now clothed in our flesh.

Because Christ has no personal subsistence except one which we acknowledge has been eternally the Son of God, we must necessarily apply to the person of the Son of God even those things which are spoken of Christ according to his human nature. For example: according to the flesh he was born of the Virgin Mary, baptized by John in the river Jordan, condemned by Pilate to die, and executed by the Jews. We cannot properly say that the Virgin bore, or that John baptized, or that Pilate condemned, or that the Jews crucified only his human nature, because these events are all attributed to him personally. His person is the subject which receives them; his nature makes his person capable of receiving. If we say that the person of a man in our Savior Christ was the subject of these things, we will obviously entrap ourselves in that same Nestorian snare. The only difference between the Nestorians and the church of God was that Nestorius imagined that Christ has both a personal human subsistence and a divine one, while the church acknowledges that Christ has both a divine and a human substance, but no other personal subsistence than the divine one. The Son of God did not take a man's person to himself, but only the nature of a man.

Christ is a person both divine and human. He is not two persons in one. Nor is he divine and human both in the same sense. He is a divine person, because he *is personally* the Son of God, and human one, because he really has the nature of the children of men. Paschasius Radbertus says that in Christ, who is both God and man, "There is a twofold substance, not a twofold person, because one person extinguishes another, but one nature cannot become extinct in another."6 The personal being which the Son of God already had did not allow the substance which he took to be personal, but his divine nature continues along with the human nature which he took. It follows, then, *contra* Nestorius, that no person was born of the Virgin but the Son of God, no person but the Son of God baptized, condemned, or crucified. This one point of Christian belief, the infinite worth of the Son of God, is the very ground of all that we believe about

---

6. This is Hooker's translation (lightly modernized) of Paschasius, *On the Holy Spirit* 2.4.

life and salvation flowing from the things which Christ either did or suffered as a man on our behalf.

(4.) Now, St. Cyril, the chief of those two hundred bishops assembled in the Council of Ephesus (where the heresy of Nestorius was condemned), had written against the Arians that the Word or Wisdom of God has *only one nature*, the eternal one to which he assumed flesh. For the Arians were of the opinion that besides God's own eternal wisdom, there is a wisdom which God created before all things, by which he might create everything else, and that this created wisdom was the Word which took flesh. In offering the metaphor of man's body and soul, however, Cyril had only intended to reinforce against Nestorius the doctrine that a visible and an invisible, a mortal and an immortal substance may be united to make one person. Over time, however, Cyril's words were taken as though it had been his drift to teach that, even as in us men there is a body and a soul, so in Christ God and man make only one nature. This is the error for which six hundred and thirty fathers condemned Eutyches in the Council of Chalcedon. For as Nestorius, teaching rightly that God and man are distinct natures, mis-inferred that these two natures cannot conjoin to make one person in Christ, so Eutyches, orthodox concerning the two natures' true personal union, unsoundly denied the ongoing difference between them. We, therefore, must warily keep a middle course, shunning both Nestorius's confusion of persons and Eutyches's later confusion of natures.

These natures have been inseparable from the moment of their first combination, and will be inseparable forever. For even when Christ's soul forsook the tabernacle of his body, his deity forsook neither body nor soul. If it had, then we could not truly hold either that the person of Christ was buried, or that the person of Christ raised itself from the dead. For the body, separated from the Word, cannot in any true sense be called the person of Christ. Nor would it be true to say that the Son of God, in raising that body, raised *himself*, if his body were not both *with* him and *of* him even during the time it lay in the sepulcher. The same must be said of his soul, or we are plainly and inevitably Nestorians. Therefore, the very person of Christ, forever one and the same, was enclosed in the grave so far as its bodily substance is concerned, while only his soul was severed from his body; his deity was still inseparably joined with both by a personal union.

CHAPTER IV

53. Christ's Two Natures

*That neither of Christ's two natures gains or loses
essential properties by their union.*

(1.) This conjunction of natures in the person of
Christ results in no abolition of natural properties
pertaining to either substance, or any transition or
transmigration from one substance into another, or
any mutual infusion of the sort that would really
cause the same natural operations or properties to
become common to both substances. Whatever is
natural to Christ's deity remains uncommunicated
to his manhood. Whatever is natural to his manhood cannot be communicated to his deity. The
true properties and operations of his deity are: to
have knowledge which it is impossible for created
natures to comprehend; to be in itself the highest

cause of all things, the wellspring of immortality and life; to have neither end nor beginning of days; to be present everywhere and enclosed nowhere; to be free from alteration and passion; to produce from itself those effects which can only proceed from infinite majesty and power. The true properties and operations of his manhood are such as Irenaeus summarizes: "If Christ," he says," "had not taken flesh from the earth itself, he would not have desired those earthly nourishments by which earthly bodies are fed. This was the nature which felt hunger after long fasting, which desired rest after hard labors, which testified to its compassion and love by tears, which groaned under the weight of its sorrow and, in the extremity of grief, even melted itself away in bloody sweat."[1] To Christ we ascribe

---

1. This is the original quotation: "If He had taken nothing from Mary, He would never have availed himself of those kinds of food which are derived from the earth, by which that body which has been taken from the earth is nourished; nor would He have hungered, fasting those forty days, like Moses and Elias, unless His body was craving after its own proper nourishment; nor, again, would John His disciple have said, when writing of Him, 'But Jesus, being wearied with the journey, was sitting [to rest]'; nor would David have proclaimed of Him beforehand, 'They have added to the grief of my wounds'; nor would He have wept over Lazarus, nor have sweated great drops of blood; nor have declared, 'My soul is exceeding sorrowful.'" Irenaeus, *Against Heresies* 3.22.2, trans. Alexander Roberts, in *The Ante-Nicene Fathers*, vol. 1, *The Apostolic Fathers: Justin Martyr, Irenaeus*, ed. Alexander

both the working of wonders and the suffering of pains. We describe him in words denoting both humility and divine glory, but we apply the former to that nature which he took of the Virgin Mary, the latter to that nature which was in the beginning.

(2.) We may not, then, imagine that the properties of the weaker nature have vanished with the presence of the more glorious nature, swallowed up in it as in a gulf. On this point we dare not listen to those who over-boldly assert that: "The nature which Christ took weak and feeble from us, by being mingled with deity, became a deified nature, so that the assumption of our substance to his was like the blending of a drop of vinegar with the huge ocean. This drop still exists, but no longer with those properties which it had when unmixed. For the instant the two natures were conjoined, all distinction and difference between them became extinct. So now we can conceive of nothing regarding the Son of God except pure deity."[2] These words [ascribed to Gregory of Nyssa] are so plainly Eutychian that I suspect they were actually written by Eutyches himself. Certainly they are far from the

_____

Roberts and James Donaldson (New York: Charles Scribner's Sons, 1903), 454.

2. Gregory of Nyssa, Epistle to Theophilus of Alexandria, in *Corpus Christianorum*, Series Graeca, 45:1276.

truth, and must necessarily give way to the better advised writings of other men. Hilary of Poitiers, for instance, says: "Jesus Christ, the Lord of majesty, [was] constituted Mediator in His own person for the salvation of the Church, and being in that very mystery of Mediatorship between men and God, Himself one person, both man and God. For He, being of two natures, united for that Mediatorship, is the full reality of each nature; which abiding in each, He is wanting in neither; He does not cease to be God because He became man, nor fail to be man because He remains forever God. This is the true faith for human blessedness, to preach at once the Godhead and the manhood, to confess the Word and the flesh."[3] Cyril is plainer: "His two natures came together with each other in an indissoluble union, without blending and without change, for his flesh is flesh and not divinity, even though his flesh became the flesh of God."[4]

---

3. Hilary of Poitiers, *De Trinitate* 9.3, trans. E. W. Watson, in *The Nicene and Post-Nicene Fathers, Second Series*, vol. 9, *Hilary of Poitiers, John of Damascus* (New York: Charles Scribner's Sons, 1899), 156.

4. Cyril of Alexandria, "Letter 45: Cyril to Succensus," in *The Fathers of the Church: St. Cyril of Alexandria Letters 150*, trans. John I. McEnerney (Washington, DC: The Catholic University of America Press, 1987), 193.

(3.) These two natures serve as causes and principles of all the things which Christ has done. Some things he does as God, because his deity alone is the wellspring from which they flow; some things as man, because they issue only from his human nature; some things jointly as both God and man, because both natures concur as the sources of those actions. For, while the properties of each *nature* cleave only to their proper nature, so that Christ cannot *naturally be* as God the same which he *naturally is* as man, both natures may very well concur to *one effect*. In that respect, Christ may be truly said to *work* the very same thing both as God and man. Let us set down this rule or principle that will suffice to decide all doubts and questions about the union of natures in Christ: between the two natures there is often a *cooperation*, always an *association*, but never any mutual *participation* by which the properties of the one are infused into the other.

(4.) This rule will help us better understand what John of Damascus has written regarding statements which seem to exchange terms between the two natures, and attribute to God things belonging to manhood and to man things which properly concern the deity of Christ Jesus. The cause of these is the *association* of natures in one subject. When we speak of Christ, there is a kind of mutual exchange in which those concrete names *God* and *Man* interchangeably take one another's place, so that it does not matter whether we say that the Son of God created the world and the Son of Man saved it by his death, or that the Son of Man created and the Son of God died to save the world—both are true and valid forms of speech. This is because when we are attributing to God what the manhood of Christ claims, or to man what his deity has a right to, we mean by the name of *God* and the name of *Man* neither the one nature or the other, but the whole person of Christ in whom both natures are joined. When the Apostle says that the Jews crucified the Lord of glory [*Ed.* 1 Cor. 2:8], and when the Son of Man on earth affirmed that the Son of Man was at that same instant in heaven [*Ed.* Jn. 3:13], we see the mutual verbal exchange mentioned above. The first attributes to God or to the Lord of glory death, impossible for a divine nature; the second attributes to man ubiquity or omnipresence, impossible for human nature. Therefore, by "the Lord of glory" we must understand the whole person of Christ, who is Lord of Glory and was indeed crucified, but not *in that divine nature* for which he is termed the Lord of Glory. Likewise, "the Son of Man" must necessarily mean the whole person of Christ, who while he was a man upon earth filled heaven with his glorious presence, but not according to that nature for which he is named "man."

Without this caution, Church Fathers whose belief was sincere and whose meaning was entirely orthodox will seem in their writings to contradict one another. Theodoret argues with great earnestness that *God* cannot be said to suffer. But by that he means Christ's *divine nature, contra* Apollinarius who held that even deity itself was passible. Cyril, contending on the other side against Nestorius, argues that whoever denies that *very God* suffered death thereby forsakes the faith. But this would be heretical, if the name of *God* in this assertion did not mean (as it does) the person of Christ, who being truly God suffered death—yet in the flesh, and not in that substance for which the name of God is given him.

CHAPTER V

54. The Glorification of Christ's Humanity

What Christ has obtained according to the flesh,
by the union of his flesh with deity.

(1.) If, as has been shown, both Christ's natures remain with their properties distinct, then (in order to better understand what each nature receives from the other) we should note that Christ is a recipient in three ways: first, as he is the Son of God; second, as his human nature has been honored by union with deity; third, as through that union with deity many eminent graces have flowed as effects into his human nature. Christ thus received the gift of eternal generation, the gift of union, and the gift of unction.

(2.) By the gift of eternal generation, Christ has received from the Father the very same substance that the Father has in and of himself. For every beginning is a father to that which comes from it; and every offspring is a son to that from which it grows. Because the Father alone is the source of deity, as the Son is not (for Christ is God by being *of God*, light by issuing *out of light*), it follows that whatever Christ has in common with his heavenly Father must be given him—but given naturally and eternally, not bestowed as a benevolent favor like the gifts of union and unction. Therefore, when the Church Fathers assert as a rule that whatever Scripture describes as received by Christ should only be applied to the manhood of Christ, this is true of everything that Christ has received *by grace*, but does not apply to what he has received from the Father by eternal nativity or birth.

(3.) The second gift, the union of deity with manhood, is by grace. Indeed, there can be no greater grace shown towards man than that God should deign to unite the person of his only begotten Son to man's nature. Because "the Father loves the Son" as man, he has "given all things into his hands" [Jn. 3:35] by uniting deity with manhood. [1] It has

---

1. Because Hooker is weaving the biblical partial quotations into his prose, we have not regularized them to the NKJV here.

"pleased" the Father that in him "all fullness should dwell" [Col. 1:19]. The "name" which Christ has "above all names" is *given* him [Phil. 2:9]. "As the Father has life in himself," the Son "has life in himself" also by the gift of the Father [Jn. 5:26]. Christ speaks of the gift by which God has made him a fountain of life (in the conjunction of the natures of God and man in his own person) when he says to the woman of Samaria, "If you knew the gift of God, and who it is who says to you, 'Give Me a drink,' you would have asked Him, and He would have given you living water" [Jn. 4:10b]. The union therefore of the flesh with deity is a gift of the highest grace and favor to that flesh. For by virtue of this grace, man is really made God; a creature is exalted above the dignity of all creatures and has all other creatures placed under it.

(4.) This wonderful union of God and man can cause no alteration in the higher nature, because for God nothing is more natural than to be unchangeable. Nor is it impossible that the Word made flesh should subsist in a different manner than before, and yet remain the same as it was in all natural qualities or properties. For the incarnation of the Son of God consists merely in the union of natures, a union which perfects the weaker nature, but does not alter the nobler nature at all. As for what the person of the Son of God has attained by

27

assuming manhood, it adds up to this: to be as (as we are) truly, really, and naturally man, and thus made capable of humbler duties than his person could otherwise have performed. All that he gained for himself was to become capable of loss and detriment for the good of others.

(5.) But is it correct to say of the incarnation of Jesus Christ that, just as our nature has in no way changed his, so his nature has left ours equally unaltered? The very purpose of his taking our nature on himself was to change it, to better its quality and to advance its condition, though not in any way to abolish the substance which he took, nor to infuse into it the natural forces and properties of his deity. Therefore, as we have shown how the Son of God by his incarnation has changed the *manner* of his personal subsistence, which was once solitary and is now joined to flesh, without altering the *nature* of God, so neither are the *properties of man's nature* so much altered by the force and virtue of that union in the person of Christ as to trespass the limits of human substance. However, this is not to say that the *state and quality* of our substance remains unaltered; on the contrary, it receives many glorious effects from its intimate union with deity. God can receive nothing from us; we have obtained much from him. For although the natural properties of deity are not communicable to man's nature, the supernatural gifts, graces, and effects of deity are.

Indeed, our flesh receives great honors in many respects from being the flesh of the Son of God. But even in that glory which we share with him—the glory we await in the kingdom of heaven—there is a difference, for his right and title to this glory is as that man of whom God is himself a part. We have a right to the same inheritance with Christ, but not the same right which he has. His is such as we cannot reach, and ours such as he cannot stoop to. Furthermore, to be the way, the truth, and the life; to be the wisdom, righteousness, sanctification, resurrection; to be the peace of the whole world, the hope of the righteous, the heir of all things; to be that supreme Head to whom all power both in heaven and in earth is given—these are not honors common to Christ with other men. They are titles above the dignity and worth of any mere man, yet true of Christ *even as man*: a man with whom deity is personally joined, and to whom deity has added those excellences which make him more than worthy of that union. Finally, since God has deified our nature not by turning it into himself, but by making it his own inseparable dwelling-place, we cannot now conceive how God should either exercise divine power or receive the glory of divine praise *without* man. For in both man is now a fellow partner of deity.

(6.) But to come to the third gift, the grace of unction: did not the parts of our nature (the human soul and body of Christ) receive any ability of operation, any virtue or quality above nature by the influence of that deity with which they were joined? As surely as the sword which is made fiery not only cuts because of its own sharpness but also burns by means of the fire's heat, so surely has the deity of Christ enabled that nature which it took from man to do more than man in this world has power to comprehend. For as Christ has imparted to his human nature everything except the bare essential properties of deity, so he has showered that nature with every perfection that it was capable of receiving, at least every perfection proper to the service for which he had graciously deigned to become man. For the beams of his deity always restrained or enlarged their operations according to whatever the parts, degrees, and duties of that mystical work which he voluntarily undertook required.

(7.) From this we may conjecture somewhat about how the powers of Christ's human soul are illuminated. For being so intimate with God, it must understand everything which God works, and must necessarily be endowed with a correspondingly universal knowledge, albeit not with the infinite knowledge proper only to deity itself. The soul of Christ, which saw in this life the face of God, was filled through the visible presence of deity with all manner of graces and virtues in that unmatchable degree of perfection, of which we read that God "has anointed [him] with the oil of gladness above [his] companions" [Heb. 1:9b].

(8.) And as God has unspeakably glorified the nobler part of our nature in Christ, so likewise he has glorified even the lower part, man's bodily substance. We must here remember what we noted before, that the degrees of deity's influence on humanity were always proportionate to God's own purposes, intents, and counsels. For in this respect, Christ's naturally corruptible body lacked the gift of everlasting immunity from death, passion, and dissolution, until God (who had given it to be slain for sin) had for righteousness's sake restored it to life with the certainty of endless continuance. Indeed, even the glorified body of Christ retained the scars and marks of its former mortality.

(9.) But should we also say that his glorious body in heaven, by virtue of his divinity, now has power to be present in any and all places at once? We do not doubt that God has exalted that body, which he was pleased to make his own, in many ways above the reach of our capacities— that body by which he has saved the world; that body which has been and is the root of eternal life, the instrument by which deity works, the sacrifice which takes away sin, the price which has ransomed souls from death, the leader of the whole army of bodies that shall rise again. For although Christ's body had its beginning from mankind, God has given it life-giving efficacy and heaven has endowed it with celestial power, that virtue from above for which all the angels of heaven adore it. And yet it continues a body, a body consubstantial (that is, of one and the same substance) with our bodies, a body of the same nature and measure which it had on earth.

(10.) In summary, there are four things which together describe the whole state of our Lord Jesus Christ: his deity, his manhood, the conjunction of the two, and the distinction between the two when joined in one. There are four principal heresies that have opposed the truth about Christ: Arians bend themselves against the deity of Christ; Apollinarians maim and misinterpret his human nature; Nestorians rend Christ asunder and divide him into two persons; Eutychians confuse in his person those natures which they should distinguish. Against them have been four famous ancient general Councils: the Council of Nicaea to define against the Arians, the Council of Constantinople against the Apollinarians, the Council of Ephesus against the Nestorians, and the Council of Chalcedon against the

Eutychians. We may summarize everything antiquity has declared regarding Christian belief and in refutation of these heresies in four words: ἀληθῶς, τελέως, ἀδιαιρέτως, ἀσυγχύτως; *truly, perfectly, indivisibly, distinctly*; the first applied to Christ being God, the second to his being man, the third to the union of both, the fourth to his still continuing as both in that union. I may truly affirm that all heresies touching only the person of Jesus Christ, whether they have arisen in recent days or in any former age, may very easily be sorted under these four headings. We conclude, therefore, that to save the world it was necessary for the Son of God to be incarnate, and for God to be incarnate in Christ in just the manner declared.

CHAPTER VI

55. Is the Incarnate Christ Omnipresent?

Of the personal presence of Christ everywhere, and in what sense it may be granted he is everywhere present according to the flesh.

(1.) We have spoken thus far about the person of Jesus Christ, his two natures, their conjunction, that which he either *is* or *does* in respect to both, and that which each nature receives from the other. God in Christ is the medicine which cures the world generally, and Christ in us is the medicine by which each of us who receive him is cured individually. For Christ's incarnation and passion are not efficacious for any man's good unless he has been made a partaker of Christ, nor can we participate in him without his presence. So we must now briefly consider *how* Christ is present, that it may become clearer how we are made partakers of Christ both in the sacraments themselves and by other means.

(2.) All things are either finite or infinite; no substance, nature, or quality can possibly be capable of both. The world and all things in it are limited, as are all the effects that proceed from them, all the powers and abilities by which they work, all that they do or may do, and all that they are. This limitation of each creature is both its perfection and its preservation. Proper measure perfects all things because every thing is for some end, and cannot accomplish a disproportionate end; excesses as well as defects are opposed to this proportion. Also, because nothing perishes except through excess or defect of that duly proportioned measure which gives it perfection, it follows that measure is likewise the preservation of all things. We may conclude from these premises, both that nothing created can possibly be unlimited or receive any accident, quality, or property to really make it infinite (for then it would cease to be a creature), and also that all creatures are limited according their own kind. So, whenever we note in them anything above their kind, it follows that this thing is not properly the creatures' own, but grows in them from a cause more powerful than they are.

(3.) As the substance of each thing is, so also is its presence. It is impossible that God should ever withdraw his presence from anything, because God's substance is itself infinite. He fills heaven and earth—although he takes up no room in either—because his substance is immaterial, pure, and so incomprehensible to us in this world that, although no part of us is ever absent from him (whose whole self is present to every particular thing), we do not discern God's presence with us further than that He *is* present. We know this firmly and certainly, partly by reason and more perfectly by faith.

(4.) Seeing, therefore, that his presence everywhere follows from an infinite and incomprehensible substance—for what can be everywhere except that which can nowhere be comprehended?—to inquire whether Christ is everywhere is to inquire about a natural property, a property that cleaves to the deity of Christ. As Christ shares this deity with no one but the Father and the Holy Ghost, it follows that nothing of Christ that is limited (nothing created, neither the soul nor the body of Christ, neither Christ as man nor Christ according to his human nature) can possibly be present everywhere. Those very phrases of limitation highlight the principal subject to which any attribute belongs, or indicate the root cause from which such an attribute grows. For example, when we say that Christ suffered death as a man (or according to his human nature), we highlight which nature was the proper subject of mortality. When we say that he conquered death as God (or according to his deity), we declare that his deity's force and virtue was the cause by which he raised himself from the grave. But the manhood of Christ is not a subject that accords with universal presence, nor is it the original cause by which his person is able to be everywhere present. Therefore, Christ is essentially present with all things because he is very God, but he is not present with all things as a man—for manhood and its parts can neither be the cause nor the true subject of omnipresence.

(5.) Nevertheless, in order to show somewhat more plainly why the manhood of Christ can neither be (nor cause his person to be) omnipresent, we acknowledge that these words of St. Augustine are entirely true: "Hence, as the Word, Christ is the Creator, for *all things were made through him* (Jn 1:3), but, as man, Christ was created."[1] It appears that no single creature has the power to be present with all creatures. But it does not actually follow that Christ cannot be omnipresent, simply because he is himself a creature. For only *infinite* presence

---

1. Augustine, *Letter 187*, in *The Works of St. Augustine: A Translation for the 21st Century*, vol. 2, *Letters 156–210*, trans. Roland Teske (New York: New City Press, 2004), 234 [8].

is irreconcilable with the essence or being of any creature. Since the whole race, mass, and body of all things that exist is still finite, Christ's creature-liness does not *per se* exclude the possibility of his presence with them all. It is only his being a *man*, a creature *of this particular kind,* that rules out om-nipresence. For the God of nature has set certain bounds of restraint and limitation to the human creature, and attributing anything beyond them to that creature would be to change its nature, to make it a creature of some other kind than in truth it is.

(6.) Furthermore, if Christ were to be omnipres-ent in his manhood—seeing as this does not come by the nature of manhood itself—it must grow by the grace of union with deity, or by the grace of unction received from deity. We have already suffi-ciently proved that, by the force of their union, the properties of both natures are imparted *only to the person* in whom they are united; what belongs to the one *nature* is not really conveyed or transfused into the other. We have also proved that the two na-tures united in Christ continue as the same natures which they are separately. And although the grace of unction (which contains the gifts and virtues which Christ the man has above other men) does make him really and habitually a more excellent man than we are, it does not take from him our nature and substance. Nor does it cause his soul or body to be of another kind than ours is. Supernatural gifts are an advancement, not an extinguishment, of that nature to which they are given. The substance of Christ's body therefore neither has, nor can have, a non-local presence. It was not therefore everywhere seen; it did not everywhere suffer death; it could not everywhere be entombed; nor is it everywhere now being exalted into heaven. All the proofs in the world that Christ had a true body depend on the true and natural properties of that body. There could be no proof in the world strong enough to convince us that Christ had a true body except according to the true and natural properties of his body. Among these properties, the chief is a definite or local presence. Tertullian writes: "But how will all this be true…if He really had not in Himself that which might be crucified, might die, might be buried, and might rise again? I mean this flesh suffused with blood, built up with bones, interwoven with nerves, entwined with veins."[2] If his majestic body now has any new property by whose power it may *in substance* be omnipresent, or even may be in many places at once, then the majesty

---

2. Tertullian, *On the Flesh of Christ* 5, trans. Peter Holmes, in *The Ante-Nicene Fathers*, vol. 1, *The Writings of Tertullian, Vol. 2*, ed. Alexander Roberts and James Donaldson (Edinburgh: T&T Clark, 1870), 174.

of his condition has extinguished the reality of his nature. St. Augustine writes: "Do not doubt, therefore, that the man Christ Jesus is now in heaven, from where he will come, and...he will come just as he was seen going to heaven, that is, in the same form and substance of the flesh, to which he certainly gave immortality, but did not take away its nature. In accord with this form he should not be thought to be spread out everywhere. For we must be careful not to defend the divinity of the man in such a way that we remove the reality of his body."[3] According to St. Augustine's opinion, therefore, if we make out that Christ's majestic body is everywhere present, then it ceases to have the substance of a true body.

(7.) To conclude, in light of the preceding arguments we hold it as a proven and infallible truth that Christ is not everywhere present as a man. There are others who think it just as infallibly true that Christ *is* everywhere present as a man.[4] To be sure, there is some sense in which we may grant this. Christ's human substance in itself is naturally absent from the earth—his soul and body are

---

3. Augustine, *Letter 187*, 235 [10].

4. Hooker here has in mind the scholastic Lutheran teaching on Christ's ubiquity in the flesh.

not on earth but only in heaven. Yet because this substance is inseparably joined to that personal Word which is present with all things by his divine essence, the human nature which cannot have universal presence in itself has it after a sort by being nowhere severed from that omnipresent divine nature. Because that infinite Word is indivisible, it could not be incarnate in part, but must necessarily be wholly incarnate. And therefore, wherever the Word is, it has manhood with it. Otherwise, the Word should be in some part or place God only and not man, which is impossible. For the person of Christ is whole, perfect God and perfect man wherever it may be, even though (since the parts of his manhood are finite and his deity infinite) we cannot say simply that the whole of Christ is everywhere, while we may say without qualification that his deity, and his person by the power of deity, are everywhere. For the actual *position* of Christ's manhood is restrained and tied to a certain place; it is only the *conjunction* with deity that extends as far as deity. Yet presence by way of conjunction is a sort of presence.

(8.) Again, just as the manhood of Christ may be said, in a sense, to be everywhere present, because Christ's manhood is nowhere severed from the divine substance of his omnipresent person, we may speak of that same universality of presence

in another respect. That is by his manhood's om-
nipresence through cooperation with deity in all
things. The light created of God in the beginning
first illuminated the world by itself; but since the
Sun and Moon were created, the world has always
enjoyed the same light *by them*. Likewise, Christ's
deity wrought all things without man before our
Lord's incarnation; but since deity assumed human
nature, that nature is never absent from or idle in
any of his works. Christ as man has all power given
to him, both in heaven and on earth. He has, not
only as God, but as man, supreme dominion over
the quick and dead (as we see in his ascension into
heaven and his sitting at the right hand of God).
The Son of God, who first humbled himself by
taking our flesh upon him, afterwards descended
much lower, and became obedient according to the
flesh all the way to suffering death, even the death
of the cross, for all men, because it was his Father's
will. The former was a humiliation of deity; the
latter was a humiliation of manhood. Therefore,
what followed was an exaltation of that humbled
humanity; for he created the world with power, but
restored it by obedience. As Christ on earth had in
his manhood glorified God by obedience, so God
has glorified in heaven that nature which was obedient. He has given Christ—even as he is a man—
such fullness of power over the whole world, that
he who previously fulfilled, humbly and patiently,

whatever God required, now reigns in glory till the restoration of all things. He who came down from heaven and descended into the lowest parts of the earth has ascended far above all heavens, so that, sitting at the right hand of God, he might from there fill all things with the gracious and happy fruits of his saving presence.

The 'ascension into heaven' is a clear local translation of Christ, according to his manhood, from the lower to the higher parts of the world. 'Sitting at the right hand of God' is the actual exercise of that rule and dominion in which the manhood of Christ is joined and matched with the deity of the Son of God. Not that his manhood lacked that power before: but the full use of it was suspended until he had laid aside that humility which previously had served as a veil to hide and conceal his majesty. After he rose again from the dead, God set him at his right hand in the heavenly places far above all principality, and power, and might, and domination, and every name that is named not only in this world but also in that which is to come. God has put all things under Christ's feet, and has appointed him as the Head of the church which is his body, that fullness of him who fills all in all. The scepter of that spiritual rule over us in this present world will at length be yielded up into the hands of the Father who gave it; that is, the use and exercise of his scepter shall cease, because there will no longer be any militant church on earth to be governed. Therefore, he exercises this government both as God and as man: as God by essential presence with all things; as man by cooperation with that which is essentially present. As for the manner by which he works in all things as a man, the principal powers of the soul of man are the will and the understanding. Christ's human will therefore assents unto all things which his deity works, and nothing which his deity works is hidden from his human understanding; thus, the soul of Christ is present by knowledge and assent with all things which his deity works.

(9.) And even the body of Christ itself—its definite limitation notwithstanding—in a sense admits of a kind of infinite and unlimited presence. For as his body is a part of that nature presently joined unto deity wherever deity is, it follows that his bodily substance has a presence of true conjunction with deity everywhere. And because it is, by virtue of that conjunction, made the body of the Son of God (by whom it was also made a sacrifice for the sins of the whole world), it has been given *a presence of power and efficacy* throughout all generations of men. Therefore, although nothing is actually infinite in substance except God only in that he is God, nevertheless as every number is infinite by possibility of addition, and every line is infinite by possibility of extension, so there is no limit which can be set to the value or merit of the sacrificed body of Christ; it has no measured certainty of limits, knows no bounds of efficacy unto life, but is itself also infinite in *possibility of application*.

Having impartially considered in every way that gracious promise of our Lord and Savior Jesus Christ concerning his presence with his own to the very end of the world, I see no reason why we cannot safely understand him to perform his works both as God by the essential presence of deity, and as man in that order, sense, and meaning which we have shown.

CHAPTER VII

56. Christ's Mystical Union with the Church

The union or mutual participation which is between Christ and the church of Christ in this present world.

(1.) We have spoken so far of the person and of the presence of Christ. "Participation" is that mutual inward hold which Christ has of us and we of him, so that each possesses the other by way of special interest, possession, and union. In order to more plainly explain this, we may derive the following two principles from what has been previously proven: "Every original cause imparts itself unto those things which come from it"; and "Anything which receives being from any other is (after a sort) *in* that which gives it being."

(2.) It follows from this that the Son of God, being light *of* light, must also be light *in* light. The persons of the Godhead, because of the unity of their substance, as necessarily remain one *within* another, as they are necessarily distinguished one *from* another—for two spring from one, and one is the offspring of the other two, and of the three only one does not grow out of any other. And since they are all only one God in number, one indivisible essence or substance, their distinction cannot possibly admit separation. For how should one subsist *solitarily* by himself, who has no substance except *individually* that very same substance whereby others subsist with him? For the multiplication of particular substances would be necessary to make things which have the same general nature subsist separately from one another, but the persons of that Trinity are not three particular substances to whom one *general* nature is common; rather they are three persons who subsist by one *substance which itself is particular*. Yet all three have it, and their individual ways of having it are what make their personal distinctions. The Father therefore is in the Son, and the Son in him; they are both in the Spirit, and the Spirit in both of them. So the Father's first offspring, who is the Son, remains eternally in the

Father, and the Father in the Son. Because of the sole and single unity of their substance, they are not severed or divided in any way. The Son is in the Father as light is in that light out of which it flows without separation; the Father is in the Son as light is in that light which it causes and does not leave. And because in this respect the Son's eternal being is of the Father—that eternal being which is his life—he therefore lives by the Father.

(3.) Again, since all things love their offspring according to the degree to which they are themselves contained in them, he who is the only-begotten must necessarily be the only-beloved of the Father. Therefore, he who is in the Father by eternally deriving his life and being from him, must also be in him through an eternal affection of love.

(4.) His incarnation means that he is also *as a man* in the Father, and the Father in him. For as he is man, he receives life from the Father as from the fountain of that ever-living deity, which in the person of the Word has combined itself with manhood, and imparts to it such life as no other creature besides him has received. For this reason also the Father necessarily loves his incarnate Son more than any other, and no other creature can match the perfection of love which Christ bears towards his heavenly Father. Therefore, God is not so in any creature, nor any creature so in God, as Christ— whether we consider him as the personal Word of God, or as the natural Son of Man.

(5.) All other things that are of God nonetheless do have God in them, and he has them in himself. Yet because their substance and his wholly differ, their coherence and communion either with him or among themselves is in no way like that union between the persons discussed above.

God pours his influence into the very essence of all things—indeed, without this influence supporting them, their utter annihilation would immediately follow. All things have received from him their first being, and their continuance in being. All things are therefore partakers of God; they are his offspring; his influence is in them. The personal Wisdom of God is thus said to excel all things in nimbleness or agility, to pierce into all intellectual, pure, and subtle spirits, to go through all, and to reach unto everything that is. Otherwise, how should his wisdom support, bear up, and sustain them all?

Whatever God works, the hands of all three persons can be found jointly and equally at work, according to *the order of that connection* by which they each depend upon the others. And therefore— although in respect to order the Father is first, the

Son next, the Spirit last and therefore the closest to every effect that all three together produce—nonetheless, since they are all of one essence, they all likewise have the same efficacy. Does any man dare (unless he is altogether ignorant of the inseparability of the persons of the Trinity) persuade himself that each of the persons may have their sole and separate possessions? Or that we, unless we are partakers of all, can have fellowship with any one? The Father as Goodness, the Son as Wisdom, and the Holy Ghost as Power all concur in every particular deed that issues from that single glorious deity which they all are. For Goodness moves God to work, and Wisdom orders his work, and Power perfects his work. All things that God has brought forth in their times and seasons were in God eternally and before all times, as a work unbegun is in the artist who afterward crafts it. Therefore, whatever we behold now in this present world was enwrapped within the heart of divine Mercy, written in the book of eternal Wisdom, and held in the hands of omnipotent Power before the first foundations of the world were laid.

All things God has made are thus the offspring of God; they are *in him* as effects are in their highest cause. He, likewise, is actually *in them*: the assistance and influence of his deity is *their life*.

The Word Made Flesh for Us

(6.) Now, if we add *saving power* to the creative power just described, it will bring forth a special offspring among men—those whom God has himself given the gracious and lovely name of sons. We are by nature the sons of Adam. When God created Adam, he created us, and as many as are descended from Adam have in themselves the root from which they spring. Some of us, though, are also sons of God—only by his special grace and favor. The sons of God have God's own natural Son as a second Adam from heaven, and are the Son's race and progeny by spiritual and heavenly birth. Therefore, as God eternally loves his Son, he must also have eternally loved in him and preferred before all others those who are spiritually descended and sprung from him. These were in God, not only as in their Creator, but also as in their Savior. The purpose of his *saving* Goodness, his *saving* Wisdom, and his *saving* Power inclined itself towards them.

(7). Those who were eternally in God by election, now truly have God in them by vocation or adoption, as the artist is in the work that his hand now frames. Life, like all other gifts and benefits, grows originally from the Father, comes to us as a race by the Son, and comes to us individually through the Spirit.[1] For this reason, the Apostle wishes for the

---

1. Cf. 1 John 5:11 and Romans 8:10.

church of Corinth, "The grace of our Lord Jesus Christ, and the love of God, and the communion of the Holy Spirit" [2 Cor. 13:14]. St. Peter describes all three together as being "The participation of divine Nature" [2 Pt. 1:4].[2] Therefore, we are eternally in God through Christ according to his eternal purpose by which he chose to make us his in this present world before the world itself was made. We are in God through his knowledge of us, and through the everlasting love he has borne towards us. But we are truly and fully in God only from the time of our actual adoption into the body of his true church, into the fellowship of his children. Because he knows and loves his church, we know that those who are in the church are in him. The fact that we are in Christ by eternal foreknowledge does not save us without our actual and real adoption into the fellowship of his saints in this present world. For we are truly in him by our actual incorporation into that society which has him for its Head, and is thus with him one Body, and in that respect shares with him one name. Thus, by virtue of this mystical conjunction, we are of him and in him even as though our very flesh and bones were made continuous with his. We are in Christ because he knows and loves us even as parts of him-

---

2. For the 2 Peter reference, we have used the ASV, which matches Hooker's syntax more closely than the NKJV here.

self; no man is actually in him but those in whom he actually is. For "he who does not have the Son of God does not have life" [1 Jn. 5:12]. Again: "I am the vine, you *are* the branches. He who abides in Me, and I in him, bears much fruit," but the branch severed from the vine withers [Jn. 15:5–6]. We are therefore adopted as sons of God to eternal life by participation with the only-begotten Son of God, whose life is the wellspring and cause of ours.

Some men argue that we are "in Christ" only in the sense that the same nature which makes us men is also in him and makes him a man like us. But this is too cold an interpretation. For what man in the world does not have this kind of communion with Jesus Christ? This cannot sustain the weight of sentences that speak of the mystery of our indwelling with Jesus Christ [Jn. 14:20; 15:4]. The church is in Christ as Eve was in Adam. Yes, by grace every one of us is in Christ and in his church, as we are by nature in our first parents. God made Eve of Adam's rib, and he frames his church out of the very flesh, the very wounded and bleeding side of the Son of man. His body crucified and his blood shed for the life of the world are the true elements of that heavenly being which makes us like himself from whom we come. For this reason we may fittingly apply the words of Adam as the words of Christ about his church—"flesh of my flesh" and "bone of my bones," a true native extract out of my own body [Gen. 2:23]. Our heavenly being grows out of his manhood even as branches grow up from their root.

He is life to all things, light to men *as the Son of God*, and both life and light eternal to the church by being made the Son of Man for us and by being in us a Savior, whether we consider him as God or as man. Adam is in us as an original cause of our nature, and a cause of that corruption of Nature which brings death. Christ is in us as the original cause of our restoration to life. Adam's person is not in us—only his nature and its corruption derived by all men through propagation. Christ has Adam's nature as we do, but incorrupt, and gives incorruption not through Adam's nature but immediately from his own person to all who belong to him. Therefore, as we are really partakers of the body of sin and death received from Adam, all that we say of eternal life is only a dream unless we are truly partakers of Christ and really possess his Spirit.

(8.) The Spirit of the second Adam brings us to life by means of his flesh. The union of his deity with our nature made our nature incorrupt in him. Thus, the sentence of death and condemnation, which only takes hold upon sinful flesh, could not possibly extend to him. This caused his voluntary death for others to prevail with God, and to have the power of an expiatory sacrifice. The blood of

Christ, as the Apostle declares, therefore takes away sin, because "through the eternal Spirit [he] offered Himself without spot to God" [Heb. 9:14]. That which sanctified our nature in Christ and made it a sacrifice powerful to take away sin, is the same which quickened it, raised it out of the grave after death, and exalted it unto glory. Seeing therefore that Christ is in us as a life-giving Spirit, the first degree of communion with Christ must consist in the participation of his Spirit, which Cyprian thus describes well as *germanissimam societatem*, that is, the highest and truest society that can be between man and him who is both God and man in one.[3]

(9.) St. Cyril, duly considering these things,[4] reproves those who taught that only Christ's deity is the vine on which we by faith depend as branches, and that neither his flesh nor our bodies are included in this metaphor. Can anyone doubt that our own bodies receive from the flesh of Christ itself that life which shall make them glorious at the last day, and for which they are already accounted parts of his blessed body? Our corruptible bodies could never live the life they shall live were they not joined here with his incorruptible body. His

---

3. Cyprian, *De Coena Dom.* c. 6.

4. Cyril of Alexandria, *Commentary on John's Gospel*, 10.13.

body is in ours as a cause of immortality—a cause by removing everything that impedes the life of our bodies through the death and merit of his own flesh. Christ is therefore, both as God and as man, that true vine of which we are both spiritually and corporeally branches. Although the ancient Fathers disclaim the mixture of his "bodily substance" with ours, they do speak of the mixture of his "flesh" with ours, in order to signify what our own bodies receive through mystical conjunction from that life-giving power which we know to be in his. They will even borrow various metaphors of bodily mixtures to declare the truth of (though not the manner of) the union between his sacred body and the sanctified bodies of the saints.[5]

(10.) No Christian man will deny that when Christ sanctified his own flesh, giving as God and receiving as man the Holy Ghost, he did this not only for himself but for our sakes, so that the grace of sanctification and life which he received first might pass from him to his whole race, as the curse came from Adam unto all mankind. But, the sanctifying work of his Spirit is prevented in us by the sin and death already possessing us, so it is necessary that both our present sanctification unto newness of life and

5. Cyprian, *De Coen. Dom.* c. 6; Irenaeus, *Against Heresies* 4.34; Cyril, *Commentary on John's Gospel* 10.13.

the future restoration of our bodies should rest first upon our participation in the grace, power, merit and virtue of his body and blood. Unless this foundation is first laid, there will be no place for those other operations of the Spirit of Christ to follow. So Christ clearly imparts himself by degrees.

It pleases him in mercy to account himself incomplete and maimed without us. But we are assured that we all receive of his fullness, because he is in us as a moving and working cause, from which flow many blessed effects in various kinds and degrees, all tending to eternal happiness. All men are partakers of Christ inasmuch as he works as Creator and providential Governor of the world; but not all are partakers of that grace by which he inhabits those he saves.

Again, just as he does not dwell in all by grace, so he does not work equally in all those whom he indwells. "And why in all the saints," says St. Augustine, "are some holier than others except by having God dwelling in them more abundantly?" And because the divine substance of Christ is equally present in all, and his human substance equally distant from all, it appears that the participation of Christ in which there are many degrees and differences must consist in the effects which are really derived from both natures of Christ into us and made our own. By having these effects in us, we can truly say that we have him from whom they come. Christ inhabits us and imparts himself more or less as the graces that really flow into us from Christ are more or fewer, greater or smaller.

Christ is whole with the whole church, and whole with every part of the church, as regards his person, which can in no way divide itself into degrees and portions. But when we speak of communion with Christ, this denotes not just the presence of his person and its mystical union with the parts and members of his whole church, but a true actual influence of grace into each of us, by which the life we live according to godliness is his, and from which we receive those perfections in which our eternal happiness consists.

(11.) We thus participate in Christ partly by imputation, as when those things which he did and suffered for us are imputed unto us for righteousness; and partly by habitual or real infusion, as when grace is inwardly bestowed while we are on earth, and afterwards both our souls and bodies are made more fully like his in glory. The first thing Christ infuses into our hearts in this life is his Spirit, on which the rest necessarily depends and from which it infallibly follows. Therefore, the Apostles sometimes term the Spirit the seed of God, sometimes the pledge of our heavenly inheritance, and sometimes the first-fruits or earnest of that which is to come [1 Jn. 3:9; Eph. 1:14; Rom. 8:23]. Because of this, those who belong to the mystical body of our Savior Christ, and are in number as the stars of heaven, divided because of their mortality into many generations, are nevertheless each coupled to Christ their head and to one another. For the same Spirit who anointed the blessed soul of our Savior forms, unites, and animates Christ's whole race as if both he and they were so many limbs compacted into one body, by being all quickened with one and the same soul.

(12.) The initial grace in which we partake of Jesus Christ by imputation is received equally and to the same degree by all who have it. Consider: this grace consists of those acts and deeds of Christ which continued only as long as he did them, and thus could belong at the time to none but him from whom they came. Therefore, it is impossible to imagine how other men could be made partakers of them—either before, during, or after Jesus' actions—except by imputation. Moreover, if a deed is to be imputed at all, then all those who have it by imputation must have it whole and entire. Therefore, since neither Christ's personal presence, nor the grace we participate in by imputation has any degrees (we have it whole or not at all), it follows that the only grace subject to degrees of participation is Christ's *infused* grace. But even here the beginning of life, the seed of God, and the first-fruits of Christ's Spirit do not admit of degrees. For by these we are given the status of sons of God, among whom (however far one may seem to excel another) because all are sons, all are equals. Some perhaps are better sons than the rest, but none is any more a son than another.

(13.) In summary, we have seen how the Father is in the Son, and the Son in the Father; how both are in all things, and all things are in them. We have seen what communion Christ has with his church: how his church and every member of it is in him by original derivation, and he personally in them by way of mystical association wrought through the gift of the Holy Ghost, which those who are Christ's receive from him, as well as whatever benefits the living force of his body and blood may yield. Yea, by steps and degrees they receive the complete measure of all such divine grace, which sanctifies and saves them all the way to the day of their final exaltation to fellowship in glory with Christ, from whom they now partake of those things tending to glory. We can say all this regarding the participation which we have with Christ without resorting to any crude notions of any mixture of the substance of his flesh with ours.

CHAPTER VIII

57. The Necessity of Sacraments

The necessity of sacraments to our participation in Christ.

(1.) It is very offensive that some people, when they labor to show the use of the holy sacraments, assign them no purpose except *to teach* the mind—by other senses—what the Word teaches by hearing. We see how easily this may lead to neglect and carelessness of such heavenly mysteries, based on our experiences with those men who most strongly entertain this opinion. For where the Word of God may be heard, it teaches anything we have to learn more efficiently and with fuller explanation than the sacraments ever will. So if the only benefit we reap from sacraments is instruction, then anyone who always has the opportunity of using the better means for that purpose will surely hold the worse in lower esteem. And indeed, would it not be superfluous to administer any sacrament to infants (who are not capable of instruction), if to administer the sacraments is only to teach the receivers what God does for them? Doubtless then there must be some other more excellent and heavenly use for the sacraments.

(2.) Sacraments, because of their mixed nature, are more debated and diversely interpreted than any other part of our faith. Because so many different properties belong here to the same thing, and every man is liable to seize upon one to the exclusion of the others, the various opinions about the necessity of sacraments seem to contradict one another, when the disagreement is not so great after all. For instance, if we focus on the duty which every communicant undertakes, we may well conclude that the main purpose of sacraments is to serve as bonds of obedience to God, strict obligations to the mutual exercise of Christian charity, provocations to godliness, preservations from sin, and memorials of the principal benefits of Christ. If we focus on the time of their institution, then it appears that God has joined them forever to the New Covenant, as other rites were previously attached to the Old. If we regard the weakness which is in us, then we will see the sacraments as warrants to strengthen our faith. If we compare those who receive them to those who do not, then the sacraments will serve as marks of distinction to separate God's own people from strangers. In all these respects, they are found to be most necessary.

(3.) But their highest power and virtue does not consist so much in all these things as in the fact that they are heavenly ceremonies, which God has sanctified and ordained to be administered in his church: first, as marks by which we know when God imparts the living or saving grace of Christ to all who are capable of receiving it; and second, as conditional means which God requires for those to whom he imparts grace. Since God in himself is invisible and we cannot see him working, when it seems good in the eyes of his heavenly wisdom that men (for some special intent and purpose) should take notice of his glorious presence, he gives them some plain and sensible token by which to know what they cannot see. It was impossible for Moses to see God and live [*Ed.* Ex. 33:20]. Yet Moses knew by fire where the glory of God was extraordinarily present [*Ed.* Ex. 24:17]. The Angel by whom God endowed the waters of the pool called Bethesda with power for supernatural healing was seen by no one [*Ed.* Jn. 5:4]. Yet the Angel's presence was known by the troubled motions of the waters themselves. The Apostles were shown by visible fiery tongues when the Spirit, whom they could not behold, was upon them [*Ed.* Acts 2:3]. It is similar with us. Although we are not able to apprehend or express how Christ and his Holy Spirit enter into the soul of man with all their blessed effects, they nonetheless give notice of the times they use to make their entry. For it pleases almighty God to communicate by sensible means those blessings which are incomprehensible.

(4.) Seeing therefore that grace is a consequence of sacraments—a thing which accompanies them as their end, a benefit which the recipient receives from God himself, the author of sacraments, and not from any other natural or supernatural quality in them—we may draw two conclusions. First, that sacraments are necessary. Second, that they are not necessary to supernatural life in just the same way that food is to natural life, because they do not contain *in themselves* any vital power or efficacy. They are not *physical* but *moral* instruments of salvation: duties of service and worship, which are unprofitable unless we perform them as the author of grace requires. For not all who receive the sacraments of grace receive the grace of God. On the other hand, it is not *ordinarily* his will to bestow the grace of the sacraments on anyone except by the sacraments. The grace that Christians receive by or with the sacraments originates from God, not from the sacraments themselves. For Solomon's wise observation about the brazen serpent also applies to the sacraments: "For he who turned toward it was saved, not by what he saw, but by thee, the Savior of all" [Wis. 16:7].[1]

(5.) The necessity of sacraments, then, is as follows. That saving grace which Christ originally is or has in himself for the general good of his whole church, he channels into each individual church member by means of sacraments. Sacraments serve as God's instruments for that end and purpose; they are moral instruments whose use is in our hands, but whose effect is in his. We have his express commandment for their use and his conditional promise for their effect, so that unless we are obedient to the former we have no apparent assurance of the latter. But where the signs and sacraments of God's grace are not contemptuously neglected or faithlessly received, we must believe that they really give what they promise, and are what they signify. We do not take baptism or the eucharist for bare resemblances or memorials of absent things, nor for naked signs and testimonies assuring us of grace received before. Rather, we take them as (and in-

---

1. Hooker here quotes from the apocryphal Wisdom of Solomon 16:7 (RSV).

deed in truth they are) effectual means by which God delivers into our hands that grace powerful unto eternal life, a grace which the sacraments thus represent or signify.

(6.) Many difficulties have grown up around the doctrine of the sacraments for want of distinct explanations about what kind or degree of grace belongs to each sacrament. Few now rightly and distinctly understand the true and direct reasons why baptism and the supper of our Lord are each necessary. To be sure, many of the same effects and benefits which come to us through the one sacrament may also be rightly attributed to the other. But baptism claims for itself only the beginning of those graces whose consummation depends on mysteries which follow. We receive Christ Jesus in baptism once as the first beginner of our life, and in the eucharist repeatedly to bring our life by degrees to its completion. By baptism, therefore, we receive Christ Jesus, and from him that saving grace which is proper unto baptism. We also receive him by the other sacrament, in which he imparts himself and that grace properly bestowed by the eucharist. So, as each sacrament has both a general or common aspect, and one particular to itself, we may conclude that the participation in Christ which properly belongs to each sacrament is not to be obtained by any other means.

CHAPTER IX

58. The Rite of Baptism

The substance of baptism; the rites or solemnities belonging to baptism; if the substance of baptism is kept, other things may be omitted when necessary.

(1.) Now, just as the soul organizes the body and gives each of its members that substance, quantity, and shape which nature deems most expedient, so the inward grace of sacraments may teach us what serves best for their outward form (which should not be neglected in any part of the Christian religion, but much less here). The grace which God intended for us by the sacraments caused him to choose for them certain outward elements, and explains why those elements are fitting vehicles of that grace. But since the grace which we here receive in no way depends upon the natural power of those visible elements, it was necessary to add words of express declaration—taken from the very mouth of our Lord himself—to these elements, that the words might infallibly teach what the signs most assuredly bring to pass.

(2.) In writing and speaking of the blessed sacraments, we typically use the word "substance" not only to refer to their outward and sensible nature, but also to the secret grace which they signify and exhibit. This is why any definitions of the sacraments, whether framed more expansively so as to increase their number or more strictly to reduce it, commonly identify grace as the sacraments' true essential form, and the elements as the matter to which form is joined. But if we separate what is hidden and consider only what is seen, as is necessary when verbally distinguishing sacraments from sacramental grace, then the name "sacrament" refers only to the *outward substance*. To complete the outward substance of a sacrament, we need an outward *form*, which the sacramental elements receive from sacramental words. For this reason, there are often said to be three things that make up the substance of a sacrament: the grace which is there offered, the element which shadows or signifies grace, and the word which expresses what is done by the element. So if we consider only the outward aspect of any sacrament, there are two essential parts; if we consider both the outward and inward substance, there are three that together give the sacraments their full being.

(3.) Furthermore, because definitions express only the most immediate and nearest parts of nature, leaving other relevant principles implied and presupposed, we must note that sacraments are only religious and mystical actions if they proceed from a sincere intent of the heart. But as we cannot know every man's private mind, we are not bound to examine each one; the known general intent of the church suffices. We may presume that he who outwardly does the work has inwardly the purpose of the church of God, unless the contrary is obvious.

(4.) All other orders, rites, prayers, lessons, sermons, actions, etc., are only accessories to the outward substance of baptism, which the wisdom of the church of Christ should order as needed. As such ordinances have been made to adorn the sacrament, the sacrament does not depend on them. They are not of the substance of baptism, which is far more necessary itself than any incidental rite or solemnity ordained for its better administration. So in a case where the fitting accompaniments of baptism are impossible, it would be better to enjoy the body of the sacrament without its adornments, than to wait for the latter and lose the opportunity for the former. Granting this, it certainly does not seem absurd (to say the least) to affirm that in cases of necessity which allow no delay for baptism to be administered with the usual solemnities, any man may tolerably receive baptism without such rites, rather than be allowed to depart this life without receiving the sacrament at all.

CHAPTER X

59. Is Baptism Necessary?

The scriptural grounds for the necessity of outward baptism.

(1.) Those who deny the possibility of such situations of necessity arising (when the church should tolerate baptism without its decent rites and solemnities) pretend that such tolerations have risen from a false interpretation that "certain men" have made of the Scripture.[1] These men, they say,

---

1. Hooker is paraphrasing Thomas Cartwright: "Private baptism first developed from a false interpretation of John 3:5, 'Unless one is born of water and the Spirit…' Certain men interpret the word 'water' as the material and elemental water, whereas our Savior Christ takes 'water' there as a metaphor for the Spirit of God, whose effect the water shadows forth. Compare this to Matthew 3:11, where by 'fire and the Spirit'

falsely ground the necessity of external baptism upon the words of our Savior Christ, "Unless one is born of water and the Spirit, he cannot enter the kingdom of God " [Jn. 3:5]. For they imagine that by "water and the Spirit" we should understand no more than if Christ had mentioned the Spirit alone without speaking of water. They think this is plain, because it seems probable elsewhere that "the Holy Ghost and fire" signifies only the Holy Ghost's work resembling fire. They conclude from this that "water," like "fire," is a metaphor for "Spirit," so Christ's words must only mean that unless one is born again of the Spirit, he cannot enter the kingdom of heaven.

(2.) I hold it as a most infallible rule in expounding Sacred Scripture, that where a literal construction will stand, the farthest from the letter is commonly the worst. There is nothing more dangerous than the licentious and deluding art that changes the meaning of words as alchemy seeks to change the

---

Christ means nothing but the Spirit of God which purges and purifies as the fire does. In this verse, then, by 'water and the Spirit' Christ means nothing but the Spirit of God which cleanses the filth of sin and cools the broiling heat of an unquiet conscience, as water washes the thing which is foul and quenches the heat of the fire" (modernized). Thomas Cartwright, *A Replye to an Answere made of M. doctor Whitgifte* (Hemel Hempstead: J. Shroud, 1573), 143.

substance of metals, makes anything what it wants it to be, and in the end brings all truth to nothing. Even if we might bear with such willful exercises of wit elsewhere, we cannot be so lax when it comes to passages that are used to ground important doctrines, as this passage does for our understanding of regeneration by water and the Holy Ghost.

(3.) In order to hide the general consent of antiquity agreeing on the literal interpretation, these wits cunningly affirm that "certain men" have taken those words as meaning material water, knowing full well that they cannot name a single ancient Father who ever expounded the passage otherwise than as implying external baptism. Shall something that has always been interpreted in only one way now be disguised as a novel invention? Must we, merely at this display of critical conceit, without more deliberation anathematize those who will not admit that "fire" in the words of John is quenched by the name of the Holy Ghost, or that "water" in the words of Christ is dried up by the name of the Spirit?

(4.) When the letter of the law has plainly and expressly specified two things—"water" as a duty required on our parts, and "the Spirit" as a gift which God bestows—there is danger in presuming to interpret it as if the clause concerning ourselves were unnecessary. By such subtle expositions, we may in the end find ourselves deemed witty but ill-advised.

(5.) Finally, consider that when that baptism of which John speaks was really and truly performed by Christ himself, we find that the Apostles (who were already baptized as we are) were baptized anew with the Holy Ghost, and received in this later baptism a visible descent of fire along with the secret miraculous infusion of the Spirit.[2] If, then, for us Christ likewise accomplishes the heavenly work of our new birth not with the Spirit alone but with water adjoining—since the most faithful expounders of his words are his own deeds—let what his hand has manifestly wrought declare what his speech doubtfully uttered.

---

2. See Acts 1:5, 2:3.

CHAPTER XI

60. Christ Commands Baptism

On the true necessity of outward baptism, gathered from the words of our Savior Christ.

1. In addition to their critique of our interpretation of John 3:5, they argue that our second oversight is to infer an over-rigorous and extreme necessity for baptism from that passage.[1] The true necessity of

---

1. "Secondly, this error [of private baptism] came from a false and unnecessary conclusion drawn from that passage. For even if the Scripture says that none can be saved except those who have the Spirit of God and are baptized with material and elemental water, this ought to be understood to refer to those who can be brought to baptism conveniently and in good order—just as the Scripture saying that he who does not believe the Gospel is condemned already (John 3:18) re-

baptism can be determined by considering a few key propositions.

First, we must consider as *necessary* all things which are either known *causes* or set *means* by which any great good is usually procured, or by which men are delivered from grievous evil. If regeneration were not in this very sense necessary to eternal life, would Christ himself have taught Nicodemus that it is impossible to see the kingdom of God except for those who are born from above [Jn. 3:3]? His words following in the next sentence—"Most assuredly, I say to you, unless one is born of water and the Spirit, he cannot enter the kingdom of God"—are a sufficient proof that his Spirit is no less necessary to our regeneration than regeneration is itself necessary to life [Jn. 3:5]. Thirdly, unless water is a necessary outward means of our regeneration just as the Spirit is a necessary inward cause, how should we read those words where we are said to be newborn ἐξ ὕδατος, that is, "of water." Why are we taught that God purifies and cleanses his church with water [Eph. 5:26]? Why do the Apostles of Christ term baptism a bath of regeneration [Tit. 3:5]? What was their purpose in advising

---

fers to those who can hear the Gospel and have discretion to understand it when they hear it. It does not condemn those who are born and remain deaf, little infants, or the mentally disabled who cannot understand what is preached" (modernized). Cartwright, *Replye*, 143.

men to receive outward baptism, and in persuading them that it availed for the remission of sins [Acts 2:38]?

(2.) If outward baptism were a cause that *in itself* possessed a kind of power (either natural or supernatural) without whose operation no new effect could possibly grow, it would follow that no man could ever receive grace before baptism (since effects never precede their necessary causes). We both know and confess that this is not true in many particular instances. For the remaining majority of people, then, although we do not make baptism a *cause* of grace, the grace which is given them *with* their baptism depends on the outward sacrament itself in such a way that God desires us to embrace it not only as a sign or token of what we receive, but also as an instrument or means by which we receive grace. For baptism is a sacrament which God has instituted in his church to the end that those who receive it may be incorporated into Christ. Thus incorporated, they obtain that saving grace of imputation, which takes away all former guilt through his most precious merit, as well as that infused divine virtue of the Holy Ghost that gives the powers of the soul their first disposition towards future newness of life.

(3.) There are some people who focus almost exclusively on the bare notion of their own eternal election as the ordinary and immediate means of grace. But predestination includes a subordination of means, without which we are not actually brought to enjoy what God has secretly intended for us. It is a self-deceiving vanity, then, to rest upon God's election if we do not ourselves keep to the ways which he has appointed for men to walk in. When the Apostle saw men called to participation in Jesus Christ, he did not fear—after they had embraced the Gospel of God and received the sacrament of life—to number them among the elect saints [Acts 2:38]. He then accounts them as delivered from death and purged clean from all sin [Eph. 5:8]. Until then, despite their preordination to life (which only God could know about), what were they in the Apostle's own account but children of wrath, aliens altogether without hope, strangers utterly without God in this present world [Eph. 2:3, 12]? Therefore, we may boldly infer from sacraments and other sensible tokens of grace that God, whose mercy condescends now to bestow the means, has long intended for us the state to which they lead. But let us never think that it is safe to presume our own final end based on bare conjectures about God's first intent and purpose, while neglecting the intermediate means. Predestination does not bring us to life without the grace of external vocation, which includes our baptism. For as we are not natural men without birth, we are not Christian men in the eyes of the church of God without new birth. Nor are we new-born, according to the manifest ordinary course of God's will, except by that baptism which both declares and makes us Christians. In this respect, we justly consider baptism the door of our actual entrance into God's house, the first apparent beginning of life—perhaps a seal to the grace of election previously received, but the first step to our sanctification here on earth.

(4.) Among the old Valentinian heretics, there were some who so admired knowledge that they ascribed everything to it. These men despised the sacraments of Christ, pretending that because ignorance had made us subject to all misery, the full redemption of the inward man and the work of our restoration must depend on knowledge alone. Those who fix their minds wholly on the acknowledged necessity of faith, and imagine that nothing but faith is necessary for the attainment of all grace, draw very near to this error. But it is a precept of our belief that sacraments are no less necessary, in their place, than belief itself. For when our Lord and Savior promises eternal life, is it any different than when he promised restitution of health to Naaman the Syrian—namely with the condition, "Wash, and be clean?" [2 Kings 5:13]. Or when he promised health to those who were stung by serpents, by beholding the brazen serpent [Num. 21:8]? If Christ who gives salvation requires baptism himself, it is not for us who look for salvation to interrogate him whether unbaptized men may be saved. It is for us to soberly do what is required, and to religiously fear the danger which may grow from omitting it. If Christ had only declared his will to have all men baptized, without teaching us any reason for baptism's necessity, our ignorance of his rationale might perhaps have made us slower to obey his command. As it is, since he has taught us that baptism is necessary to take away sin, how can we claim to have the fear of God in our hearts if we do not care enough about delivering men's souls from sin to use all possible means for their baptism? Even Pelagius, who utterly denied the guilt of original sin and the necessity of baptism in that respect, still baptized infants and acknowledged that their baptism was necessary for "entrance into the kingdom of God."[2]

(5.) Now the law of Christ, which for these reasons makes baptism necessary, must nonetheless be construed and understood according to rules of natural equity. Indeed my opponents recognize as much when they expound the passage "that he who

---

2. Quotation from Eusebius Gallicanus, *Homily 5 on Easter*, in *Corpus Christianorum*, Series Latina, 101:203.

does not believe the Gospel is condemned already." They say it only "refers to those who can hear the Gospel and have discretion to understand it when they hear it," but "does not condemn those who are born and remain deaf, little infants, or the mentally disabled."[3] Natural equity teaches them to interpret the law of Christ in this way. And all gladly confess equity's teaching that in certain cases men may receive spiritual life by virtue of an inward baptism, even without the outward sacrament. So any debate on this subject concerns not whether this is possible, but only the bounds and limits of this possibility.

For example, it would be almost barbarous to think that a man who was prevented from baptism by the crown of martyrdom would thus lose the happiness enjoyed by so many thousands who only have the grace to believe and not the honor to seal the testimony of belief with death.

Again, in St. Bernard's time certain opinionated men began to privately hold that, because our Lord has said "unless one is born of water," life cannot *possibly* be obtained at the hands of God without either actual baptism or martyrdom instead of baptism. Bernard declared himself an enemy to this severity and strictness, which only allowed an exception for martyrs. For he considered that the

---

3. See the quotation from Cartwright in fn. 28 above.

same principle of equity which had moved those men to affirm that unbaptized martyrs could be saved, should equally guarantee the salvation of those who, although lacking the sufferings of the holy martyrs, have the same virtues which sanctified those sufferings and made them precious in God's sight. "If," Bernard says, "he should have second thoughts before the end, and want and ask to be baptized, but, forestalled by death, fail in the obtaining, so long as true faith, devout hope, and unfeigned love are present and only water is lacking—may God forgive me—I am quite unable to despair of this man's salvation, nor will I believe his faith empty, crush his hope or prune away his charity: this on condition that he does not spurn the water, but is prevented by the impossibility that I have just mentioned."[4]

"Tell me," says Ambrose, "what else is in your power other than the desire, the request?…Grant, therefore, O holy Father, to Thy servant the gift…. Grant, I pray, to Thy servant Valentinian the gift which he longed for, the gift which he requested…." (For the emperor Valentinian died before his purpose to receive baptism could take effect.)

---

4. Bernard of Clairvaux, "Letter 77: To Master Hugh of Saint Victor," in *Bernard of Clairvaux: On Baptism and the Office of Bishops*, trans. Pauline Matarasso (Kalamazoo, MI: Cistercian Publications, 2004), 157 [II.6].

"He who had Thy Spirit, how has he not received Thy grace? Or if the fact disturbs you that the mysteries have not been solemnly celebrated, then you should realize that not even martyrs are crowned if they are catechumens, for they are not crowned if they are not initiated. But if they are washed in their own blood, his piety and his desire have washed him, also."[5]

It has therefore been constantly held as most equitable—for other believers as well as for martyrs—that if actual baptism is prevented by some necessity, the desire for baptism may take its place in God's eyes.

(6.) Many have harshly judged the case of infants who die unbaptized with neither the sacrament nor any conscious idea of it. But let us once more recall that grace is not absolutely tied to the sacraments; God in his kindness does not bind any no man to things altogether impossible, but when we cannot do what is commanded, he accepts our will to obey in place of the deed itself. Again, recall that Christian parents and the church of God presumably desire and intend that the sacrament of baptism should be given to these infants. In light of these

---

5. St. Ambrose, *On Emperor Valentinian*, trans. Roy J. Deferrari, in *Funeral Orations by Saint Gregory Nazianzen and St. Ambrose*, ed. Joseph Deferrari, 287–88 [51–53].

considerations, a compassionate sense of equity has moved many of the scholastic divines to grant that the all-merciful God imputes to those who are themselves unable to desire baptism the secret desire that others have on their behalf. God accepts that desire as theirs, the schoolmen say, rather than casting away their souls for something that no man can help.[6]

And in such cases, the very fact that they have been born to Christian parents may serve as a just argument that God wills to impart his grace to infants lacking baptism. Thus we approve the charitable presumption that salvation is very likely for those who have received the benefit of Christian parents, even if the Christian upbringing that should follow is prevented by a tragedy that no one can prevent. For God plainly teaches us that the seed of faithful parents is holy from the moment of birth [1 Cor. 7:14]. Now, we should not understand this as if the children of believing parents were without sin, or as if grace were derived from baptized parents merely through natural birth, or as if God had covenanted and promised to save anyone merely out of regard for their parents' belief. And yet God freely gives to all who profess the name of

_____

6. The OUP critical edition, edited by Stephen McGrade, includes citations to such Roman Catholic scholastics as Jean Gerson, Thomas Cajetan, and Gabriel Biel.

Christ a privilege which unbelievers do not receive: that the fruit of their bodies brings with it into the world a kind of birthright to those means which Christ has ordained to sanctify his church. Thus we should not think that he, who from heaven has apparently destined holiness for them by special privilege of their very birth, will himself deprive them of regeneration and inward grace only because necessity deprives them of outward sacraments. In cases, then, when we lack that beautiful visibility of baptism, it is the part of charity to hope and to judge with charity rather than cruelty.

(7.) There is, then, a necessity of receiving and a necessity of administering the sacrament of baptism. The first is perhaps not so absolute as some have thought, but the second is if anything more rigid. Should the church, called to be a mother to those who crave at her hands the sacred mystery of their new birth, repel them and see them die with their spiritual desires unsatisfied, rather than give them their souls' rights, even if it means omitting those things that serve only for more convenient and orderly administration?[7] Consider: we grant on the

---

7. "It is questionable whether there is any such necessity of baptism that the common decent orders should be broken in administering it" (modernized). Thomas Cartwright, *The Rest of the Second Replie Agaynst maister Whitgiftes Second Answer* (Heidelberg: M. Schirat, 1577), 218.

one side that those statements of Holy Scripture which make sacraments most necessary to eternal life do not threaten the salvation of those who lack them because of some inevitable necessity and through no fault of their own. But we must on the other side reasonably acknowledge that our Lord himself makes baptism necessary—both as regards the good received from baptism and the testimony of humility and meek obedience that we show to God by receiving it. Reposing entirely on the absolute authority of his commandment and on the truth of his heavenly promise, our obedience does not doubt that it will obtain grace of inestimable value even from such lowly creatures—or rather, receive grace from God, but through these creatures as his appointed means. However it may be that God saves without baptism through the secret ways of his own incomprehensible mercy, the church is not cleared from bloodguilt if through her superfluous scrupulosity she withholds the momentous grace of baptism on account of trivial impediments. Such merciless strictness may greatly harm us, if not those to whom we show it. We may perish for the hardness of our hearts, though they live through God's unspeakable mercy. God, who did not afflict the innocent boy whose circumcision Moses had too long deferred, took revenge on Moses himself for that dangerous negligence [Ex. 4:24]. He thus teaches us that those whom God's own mercy saves without us, are still destroyed as far as we are concerned, when (under insufficient pretenses) we defraud them of such ordinary outward helps as we owe them. We do not have a set day for baptism, as the Jews had for circumcision. Nor do we have a place appointed for it by God's law, but only by the church's discretion. Therefore, according to the law of Christ, baptism belongs to infants who are capable of receiving it from the very instant of their birth. And if the church postpones baptism because the time, place, or some other circumstance does not coincide solemnly enough, and the infants lose it, then the church has (as much as lies in her) willfully cast away their souls.

Editorial note: *At this point, Hooker includes a long discussion of a variety of debates in the late sixteenth-century Church of England about how, when, and where to perform baptisms. As these will primarily be of interest to the professional historian, we have omitted Chapters 61–65.*

CHAPTER XII

66. The Rite of Confirmation

Of confirmation after baptism.

(1.) It was the church's ancient custom to add the laying-on of hands after baptism, along with an effectual prayer for the illumination of God's most Holy Spirit, in order to confirm and perfect what the Spirit's grace had begun in baptism. For our prayers are our means to obtain the graces which God gives—both for ourselves and for others. When we pray for others, we bless them, because our prayer procures God's blessing on them. This is especially true of those whom God particularly regards for their piety and zeal in prayer, and of those whose place and calling gives them this duty to bless through prayer—for instance, biological and spiritual fathers.

Every age has used the laying-on of hands with prayers of spiritual and personal benediction, as a ceremony which shows our specific desires on behalf of the person we present to God in prayer. Thus, when Israel blessed Joseph's sons Ephraim and Manasseh, he laid his hands on them and prayed: "God, before whom my fathers Abraham and Isaac walked, the God who has fed me all my life long to this day, the Angel who has redeemed me from all evil, bless the lads" [Gen. 48:15–16.] The prophets, who healed diseases by prayer, used the same ceremony. So when Elisha wanted Naaman to wash himself seven times in the Jordan to cure his foul disease, Naaman was very offended, and said: "Indeed, I said to myself, 'He will surely come out to me, and stand and call on the name of the Lord his God, and wave his hand over the place, and heal the leprosy'" [2 Kings 5:11]. The same thing was usually done when men were consecrated and ordained to divine vocations, from the time of Moses to Christ. Indeed, the prayers of those who came to Christ for help were often expressed in words that make it clear that Christ himself observed this custom. He who did such great works of mercy to restore a body's health through prayer and the laying-on of hands, was also considered able to infuse heavenly grace into those whose youth was not yet depraved with malice to resist God's grace to them.

So they brought young children to him, that he might lay his hands on them and pray.

(2.) After the ascension of our Lord and Savior Jesus Christ, his Apostles continued in their daily practice what Christ had begun. Their prayer and laying-on of hands was a means by which thousands became partakers of the wonderful gifts of God. Christ had promised the church that those who believed in him would exhibit the following signs and tokens: "In my name they will cast out demons; they will speak with new tongues; they will take up serpents; and if they drink anything deadly, it will by no means hurt them; they will lay hands on the sick, and they will recover" [Mark 16:17–18]. This power was at first common to all believers, but they did not all have the power to communicate or pass it on to all other men. Those who were God's instruments to instruct, convert, and baptize new believers received the gift of miraculous operations by the power of the Holy Ghost only through the Apostle's hands. For this reason, when Simon Magus perceived that this power was in none except the Apostles and presumed that those who had it might sell it, he sought to purchase it from them with money [*Ed.* Acts 8:9–25].

(3.) These miraculous graces of the Spirit continued after the Apostles' times, as Irenaeus writes:

Wherefore, also, those who are in truth of His disciples, receiving grace from Him, do in His name perform miracles, so as to promote the welfare of other men, according to the gift which each one has received from Him. For some do certainly and truly drive out devils, so that those who have thus been cleansed from evil spirits frequently both believe in Christ, and join themselves to the Church. Others have foreknowledge of things to come: they see visions, and utter prophetic expressions. Others still, heal the sick by laying their hands upon them, and they are made whole. Yea, moreover, as I have said, the dead even have been raised up, and remained among us for many years. And what shall I more say? It is not possible to name the number of the gifts which the Church, scattered throughout the whole world, has received from God, in the name of Jesus Christ, who was crucified under Pontius Pilate, and which she exerts day by day for the benefit of the Gentiles, neither practicing deception upon any, nor taking any reward from them on account of such miraculous interpositions. For as she has

received freely from God, freely also does
she minister to others.[1]

As long as it pleased God to continue these miraculous gifts and graces in his church, it appears that
no one except bishops (the Apostles' successors for
a time, even in this power) ever made others partakers of them through prayer and the laying-on
of hands. St. Augustine acknowledges that these
gifts were not permitted to last forever, so that men
might not grow cold at the commonness of graces
whose strangeness at first inflamed them.[2] But his
account of the passing of these ordinarily occurring
miracles in no way casts doubt on those extraordinary graces more rarely observed in Augustine's day
or afterward.

(4.) Now, while the Apostles' successors had the
power to bestow the Holy Ghost by prayer and the
laying-on of hands only for a time, the rite of confirmation by these means has always continued be-

---

1. Irenaeus, *Against Heresies* 2.32.4, in *The Ante-Nicene Fathers*, 1:409.

2. It is not clear what particular Augustine reference Hooker
has in mind here. In his homily on 1 John 3:19–4:3, Augustine refers specifically to the post-apostolic cessation of the
gift of tongues. However, in *City of God* XXII.9–10, he de-
fends the ongoing reality of miracles.

cause of the very special benefits which the church thus enjoys. The Fathers everywhere ascribe to confirmation that gift or grace of the Holy Ghost—not which first makes us Christian men—but which assists us Christians in all virtue and arms us against temptation and sin. For after the administration of baptism, Tertullian says,

> In the next place the hand is laid on us, invoking and inviting the Holy Spirit through the words of benediction.... Then, over our cleansed and blessed bodies willingly descends from the Father that Holiest Spirit: over the waters of baptism, recognising as it were His primeval seat, He reposes.[3]

St. Cyprian, speaking more particularly of that work of the Spirit which was especially associated with confirmation, says:

> How great is this empire of the mind, and what a power it has [he means through baptism] not alone that itself is

---

3. Tertullian, *On Baptism* 8, trans. S. Thelwall, in *The Ante-Nicene Fathers*, vol. 11, *The Writings of Tertullian, Vol. 1*, ed. Alexander Roberts and James Donaldson (Edinburgh: T&T Clark, 1872), 239, 240.

withdrawn from the mischievous associations of the world, as one who is purged and pure can suffer no stain of a hostile irruption, but that it becomes still greater and stronger in its might [through prayer and the laying-on of hands] so that it can rule over all the imperious host of the attacking adversary with its sway![4]

Eusebius Emesenus says much the same thing: "The Holy Ghost which descendeth with saving influence upon the waters of baptism doth there give that fulness which sufficeth for innocency, and afterwards exhibiteth in confirmation an augmentation of further grace."[5] The Fathers, in short, were persuaded that confirmation was an apostolic ordinance which would always be profitable in God's church, although its external effects might not always be as striking as those signs which accompanied and certified it in apostolic times.

---

4. Cyprian, *The Epistles of Cyprian*, Epistle 1, c. 5., trans. Ernest Wallace, in *The Ante-Nicene Fathers*, vol. 5, *Hippolytus, Cyprian, Caius, Novatian, Appendix*, ed. Alexander Roberts and James Donaldson (New York: Charles Scribner's Sons, 1903), 276. Text in parentheses are Hooker's comments on Cyprian.

5. Eusebius of Emesa, *Sermon on Pentecost*, in *Corpus Christianorum*, Series Latina, 101:38.

(5.) Baptism and confirmation most commonly went together in the beginning, but were later
separated for several reasons. Sometimes this was
because the minister was of a lower rank or degree,
and could baptize but not confirm. This happened
when Peter and John confirmed people previously
baptized by Philip [Acts 8:12–15]. St. Jerome says
of a similar case: "I do not deny that it is the practice
of the Churches in the case of those who living far
from the greater towns have been baptized by pres-
byters and deacons, for the bishop to visit them,
and by the laying on of hands to invoke the Holy
Ghost upon them."[6] He continues that the faithful
in Samaria "had been baptized" and so "when the
Apostles Peter and John came, only hands were im-
posed on them, that they might receive the Holy
Ghost....which now too is done among us, so that
they who are baptized in the Church are brought to
the prelates of the Church, and by our prayers and
by the imposition of hands obtain the Holy Spirit,
and are perfected with the Lord's seal."[7] It appears,

---

6. Jerome, *The Dialogue against the Luciferians* 9, trans. W. H.
Fremantle, in *The Ante-Nicene Fathers*, vol. 11, *St. Jerome: Let-
ters and Select Works*, ed. Philip Schaff and Henry Wace (New
York: The Christian Literature Company, 1893), 324.

7. Cyprian of Carthage, *Epistle 72* 9, trans. Ernest Wallace,
in *The Ante-Nicene Fathers*, vol. 8, *The Writings of Cyprian*,
ed. Philip Schaff and Henry Wace (Edinburgh: T&T Clark,
1870), 264–65.

then, that when the baptismal ministers were of a lower order, the bishops would later confirm those baptized by them.

(6.) Sometimes those whose ecclesiastical vocation should have allowed them both to baptize and confirm were heretics excommunicated from the fellowship of true believers. There was a hot contention in some churches about how to admit into the bosom of the true church anyone initially baptized and confirmed by those heretics, but who later came to see and renounce the heretics' errors. The standard practice was to receive these converts by the laying-on of hands and prayer, not by rebaptism. Some people imagined that this was because heretics might give the remission of sins by baptism, but that they could not give the Spirit by the laying-on of hands because they did not have God's Spirit themselves. So, they reasoned, a baptism received from a heretic might stand, but confirmation must be given again. Cyprian went so far as to oppose the standard practice because of the foolishness of this explanation. He labored in many ways to prove that in the hands of heretical ministers, both the waters of baptism and the anointing oils of confirmation came to nothing. Jerome, on the other hand, combatted the error of the Luciferians, who accepted the baptism of heretics but not their confirmations and consecrations because, they said, 'Heretics cannot give the Holy Ghost.' Jerome proved that if baptism by heretics can effect the remission of sins (a grace that no man receives without the Spirit), then the same must hold for confirmation, and the church should admit converts from heresy without a new laying-on of hands.

But, some might object: "If the gift of the Holy Ghost always joins itself to true baptism, would that not imply that the church errs in holding that a bishop's confirmation is necessary to obtain the Holy Ghost?" St. Jerome answers that we observe this practice, not because it is absolutely impossible to receive the Holy Ghost by the sacrament of baptism unless a bishop afterwards lays on his hands, but because it is fitting to honor the prelacy in this way. For the safety of the church depends on the dignity of her chief superiors, and if some uniquely powerful offices were not given them, there would be as many schisms in the church as there are priests. His opinion, then, appears to have been that the Holy Ghost is received in baptism, and that confirmation is only a sacramental complement. Following from this, he concluded that the reason why only bishops ordinarily confirmed was not that there is a greater benefit, grace, and dignity in confirmation than in baptism. Rather, he argued, since the sacrament of baptism admits men into God's church, it was both reasonable and convenient that if the bishop did not baptize them, they should seek this complementary ceremony from his hands. They did this to honor the bishop's primary spiritual authority and charge over their souls; for to bless is an act of authority [Heb. 7:7].

Now, St. Jerome says nothing in that passage about the *effects* of confirmation (whether given after a heretical baptism or otherwise). This is because all men understood that in those converting from heresy, confirmation tended to the fruits of repentance, and begged the same grace on behalf of the penitent that David desired from God's hands after his fall [Ps. 51:10–12]. As for others receiving the rite, we have already discussed its fruits and benefits for them.

(7.) The final reason for separating confirmation from baptism came in the case of the baptism of infants. Although certainly able to be received into the life of the family, they were not yet old enough to be able to fight in the army of God, to discharge the duties of a Christian man, to bring forth the fruits of the Spirit, and to do the works of the Holy Ghost. For this reason, so long as baptism itself was not delayed, deferring the date of confirmation could do no harm but rather good. Because of this, children, in preparation for confirmation, were seasoned with the principles of true religion before malice and corrupt examples depraved their minds. A good foundation was thus laid early for the direction of the course of their whole lives, and the seed of the church of God was preserved sincere and sound. Then the prelates and fathers of God's family, to whom the care of these souls belonged, saw in their examination of the children a part of their own heavy burden already performed.[8] They reaped comfort from beholding the first beginnings of true godliness in tender years, glorified the God whose praise they found in the mouths of infants, and did not neglect so fitting an opportunity to give each one fatherly encouragement and exhortation. Add the laying-on of hands and prayer to this practice, and our warrant for its great good effects is the same which the patriarchs, prophets, priests, Apostles, Fathers, and men of God had for their own particular invocations and benedictions. I suppose that no man who professes the truth of religion will be quick to think those fruitless.

(8.) No, there is no reason to doubt the benefit of confirmation; but there surely is great reason to complain of the deep neglect of this Christian duty by almost all our bishops. Let them not take offense—what I say is true, and their small regard

---

8. *Ed.* Hooker is referring to the common practice of the bishop quizzing those seeking confirmation to ensure that they had been properly catechized by their parents or godparents.

for this duty has done harm in the church of God. It may happen that even after those errors rashly uttered in disgrace of this ceremony have been sponged out,[9] those which have grown through neglect of it may still remain.

---

9. "Tell me why we should have any such thing as confirmation in the church, which was brought in by the spurious decretals of the Popes" (modernized). Cartwright, *Replye*, 199. [Hooker: Cartwright retracts this claim in *The Rest of the Second Replie*, where he writes: "I concede that confirmation is more ancient than the spurious decretal epistles." Cartwright continues: "There is not a single mention of confirmation to be found in Scripture. Seeing that it is unnecessary and has been so horribly abused, why should it not be utterly abolished? Thirdly, confirmation itself has many dangerous points in it. The first step of popery in this confirmation is the laying-on of hands upon the head of the child, which confirms the general opinion that it is a sacrament. This is especially because the confirmation prayer says that this is done according to the apostles' example, which is a manifest untruth taken from the popish ritual. The second step is that the so-called 'Bishop' is the only one who may administer it, thus confirming the popish opinion that esteems confirmation above baptism. For if baptism may be ministered by the minister, but confirmation only by the bishop, there is great reason to suspect that baptism is not so precious as confirmation; this was one of the principle causes for the establishment of that wicked opinion in popery. I say nothing here of the inconvenience and expense of bringing children ten miles for something that, if it were necessary, might be just as well done at home in men's own parishes. The third step of popery is when the book [i.e., the Book of Common Prayer] says that a purpose of confirmation is that children may receive strength

(9.) The above, then, may serve as an answer to those who demand, "Tell me why we should have any such thing as confirmation in the church." For we are not ignorant of how earnestly they have protested against it, or how directly (although by their own concession untruly) some of them have said that it was instituted by the "spurious decretals of the Popes," and asked why it should not be "utterly abolished" seeing that "there is not a single mention of confirmation to be found in Scripture"— unless, of course, the Epistle to the Hebrews is Scripture [Heb. 6:2]. Seeing also that, no matter how free from abuses confirmation is now, if we look to the past (which wise men always respect more than the present)[10] it *has been* abused, it must not be such a profitable ceremony as the whole silly church of Christ has imagined (through lack of experience) for the space of these past sixteen hundred years. And that's not to mention the cruelty to poor country people, who are sometimes forced to

---

and defense against all temptations by the laying-on of hands and prayer. In reality, there is no promise that any such gift shall be given the children by the laying-on of hands. The book maintains the popish distinction that the Spirit of God is given at baptism for the remission of sins, and in confirmation for strength." Cartwright, *Second Replie*, 232].

10. *Ed.* Hooker is drawing attention to the irony of Cartwright's appeal to the past, given what he views as Cartwright's persistent antitraditionalism.

let their plows stand still and wander over mountains and through woods by the incredibly wearisome toil of their feeble bodies, nearly "ten miles" sometimes, we are told, for a bishop's blessing that, "if it were necessary, might be just as well done at home in men's own parishes." Seeing all this, they would utterly abolish the ceremony to save these poor people from purchasing a blessing with such great loss and intolerable pain.

In addition to all this they make three grievous complaints about confirmation itself. The first is that this "laying-on of hands" is said to be done "according to the Apostles' example," but that this is a "manifest untruth"—for the whole world knows that the Apostles never laid hands on anyone after baptism, and that St. Luke is much deceived when he says that they did [Acts 8:15–17]. Furthermore, our practice teaches men to think the laying-on of hands "a sacrament," presumably because it is a principle grafted by the universal light of nature into the minds of men that anything done according to apostolic example must necessarily be a sacrament. The second high point of danger is that by tying confirmation only to the bishop, "there is great reason to suspect that baptism is not so precious as confirmation." (For who could imagine that a velvet coat costs more than a linen cap, seeing that the first is an ordinary garment, while the second is an ornament only worn by a Sergeant-at-law?) Finally, to draw to the end of these perils, the last and weightiest danger is that the Book of Common Prayer itself says that "children may receive strength and defense against all temptations by the laying-on of hands and prayer." This speech of the book is a double-edged sword that dangerously wounds two ways. First, it ascribes grace to the laying-on of hands, when in reality we can no more assure ourselves of any "promise" from God that his heavenly grace will be given us, than could the Apostle that he should himself obtain grace by the bowing of his knees to God [Eph. 3:14]. Second, by using the word "strength" here (a word so apt to spread infection), we "maintain" with "popish" evangelists an old outworn "distinction" between the Holy Ghost bestowed upon Christ's Apostles before his ascension into heaven [Jn. 20:22], and augmented upon them afterwards at Pentecost [Acts 1:8]. This is a distinction of grace infused into Christian men by degrees: planted in them at first by baptism, afterward cherished, watered, and (be it spoken without offense) strengthened not only by other virtuous duties which piety and true religion teach, but also by this very special benediction of which we speak, the rite or ceremony of confirmation.

CHAPTER XIII

67. The Eucharist

Of the sacrament of the body and blood of Christ.

(1.) The grace that we receive by the holy eucharist does not begin life, but continues it. No man receives this sacrament before baptism, because no dead thing is capable of nourishment. That which grows must necessarily first live. If our bodies did not daily digest and discard food, it would be superfluous to eat again and refresh them. And it may be that the grace of baptism would serve unto eternal life, if our spiritual state were not so hindered and impaired every day after our baptism. In the life to come, then, where neither body nor soul can decay, our souls will no more require this sacrament than our bodies will need physical nourishment. But as long as the days of our warfare last, as long as our souls are prone to the weakening or renewal of grace within us, the words of our Lord and Savior Christ will stand: "[U]nless you eat the flesh of the Son of Man and drink His blood, you have no life in you" [Jn. 6:53b]. Therefore, since eternal life is the end which all men seek, those who have laid the foundation and reached the first beginning of new life in baptism find here in the eucharist the nourishment and food that ensures the continuation of this life in them. Those who desire to live the life of God must eat the flesh and drink the blood of the Son of Man, for without this diet, we cannot live. In our infancy, we were incorporated into Christ and received the grace of his Spirit by baptism without any sense or feeling of the gift which God was bestowing. But now in the eucharist we receive the gift of God in such a way that we know (by grace) what grace it is that God is giving us. We can see and judge the degrees of our own increase in holiness and virtue. We understand that the strength of our life begun in Christ is Christ—that his flesh and blood are truly and not imaginarily meat and drink. Through faith we truly perceive the very taste of eternal life in the body and blood sacramentally presented, discerning that the grace of the sacrament is as truly present as is the food which our mouths eat and drink.

(2.) Some men greatly feared that Zwingli and Oecolampadius would lead men to think of this sacrament as only a destitute shadow, empty and void of Christ. But so far as I can tell, opening up the various opinions to debate has led all sides at last to a general agreement concerning the only thing that matters—namely, our *real participation* in Christ and in the life of his body and blood *by means of this sacrament.* Why, then, should the world continue to be distracted and torn apart by so many fights, when the only remaining controversy is *where* Christ is? In fact, even on this point no side denies that the *soul of man* is the receptacle of Christ's presence. So the question is driven to an even narrower issue, with the only doubt being whether (when the sacrament is administered) Christ is wholly present *only* within man, or whether his body and blood are *also* externally seated in the consecrated elements. Those who defend the latter opinion are driven either to "consubstantiate" and incorporate Christ *with* the sacramental elements, or to "transubstantiate" and change the substance of those elements *into* his. The first holds that Christ is really but invisibly enclosed within the substance of those elements; the second hides him under a mere outward appearance of bread and wine, whose real substance (they imagine) is abolished while Christ's substance fills the same space.

(3.) All things considered, and given the hard-fought victory of truth over error on the essential point, I should wish that men would spend more time meditating with silence on *what* we have by the sacrament, and less on disputing about *how*. If any man thinks this simple-minded, let us see whether or not the Apostles of our Lord themselves followed this course. We see many examples of them having very scrupulous and inquisitive dispositions, always liable to ask questions about other less important and difficult cases. Why is it that, when so few words were uttered about so high a mystery as the eucharist, they received the gift of Christ with gladness and expressed no doubts or scruples? The explanation is clear to anyone who has ever observed how the powers of the mind are wont to stir when we behold that which we infinitely long for, above and beyond our expectation. Curious and intricate speculations hinder, abate, and quench those inflamed motions of delight and joy which divine graces raise when extraordinarily present to us. The mind that feels such present joy is always unwilling to admit any other thought, and will lay off any disputes that at other times would easily draw the intellect. For instance, compare our Lord's disciples in John 20 with the people who are said to have gone after him to Capernaum in John 6. These people had left him on one side of the Sea of Tiberias and found him again on the other as soon as they arrived there themselves by ship. But they knew that he had not come by ship himself, and that the journey over land would take longer than the time he had had to travel. They wondered, and so asked: "Rabbi, when did you come here?" [Jn. 6:25]. But when Christ appeared to his disciples in a far stranger and more miraculous manner in John 20, they asked no questions but rejoiced greatly in what they saw. Why? The first group beheld in Christ something that they knew was more than natural, but which did not enrapture their affections with any extraordinary gladness. When the second group looked on Christ, they knew that they saw the wellspring of their own everlasting felicity. The former, because they did not enjoy, disputed. The latter did not dispute, because they enjoyed.

(4.) If the presence of Christ with these disciples moved them so much, judge what their thoughts and affections must have been at the time of this new presentation of Christ—not before their eyes but within their souls. They had already learned that his flesh and blood are the true cause of eternal life—that they are the cause not by the mere strength of their own substance, but through the dignity and worthiness of the person who offered them up as a sacrifice for the life of the whole world. They knew that he still makes his flesh and blood effectual for that life, and that they are our life in particular when we receive them. But they did not yet perfectly understand what the outcome of these things would be, until they assembled (they imagined) merely to eat the Passover appointed by Moses. Then they saw their Lord and Master, with his hands and eyes lifted up to heaven, bless the chosen elements of bread and wine and consecrate them for the endless good of all generations till the world's end. The virtue of his divine benediction made these elements the instruments of life forever. These disciples were the first to be commanded to receive these gifts from the Lord; the first who were promised that these mysteries would serve (not only at the present moment but also whenever they and their successors properly administered them) as conduits of life and vehicles of his body and blood for them. Was it possible for them to hear that voice saying, "Take, eat; this is my body—Drink ye all of this; this is my blood," while they obeyed the command and believed the promise, and not be filled with a fearful wonder at the heaven which they saw within themselves as the promise was immediately fulfilled? They were wading in a sea of comfort and joy, which teaches us that this heavenly food is given us to satisfy our thirsty souls, and not to exercise of our curious and subtle wits.

(5.) If we doubt what those wonderful words mean, let us take someone as a teacher of Christ's meaning for whom Christ himself was the schoolmaster. Let our Lord's Apostle be his interpreter, and content ourselves with his explanation: "My body: 'the communion of my body.' My blood: 'the communion' of my blood" [1 Cor. 10:16]. Is there anything more straightforward, clear, and easy than this—that just as Christ is called "our life" because through him we obtain life, so the elements of this sacrament are called his "body and blood" because through them we receive his body and blood? The bread and cup are his body and blood because they are the instrumental causes, when we receive them, of our participation in his body and blood. For it is neither vain nor improper to call something that certainly produces any effect by the name of that effect itself. The person of Christ is the cause, the quickening of our souls and bodies to eternal life is the effect, and his body and blood are the true wellsprings from which this life flows. Christ's body and blood do not merely minister life to us in a way analogous to the influence of the heavens on plants, beasts, men, etc., but also by a far more divine and mystical union which makes us one with him even as he and the Father are one.

(6.) Therefore, the real presence of Christ's most blessed body and blood should not be looked for in the sacrament, but in the worthy receiver of the sacrament. The very order of our Savior's words agrees with this: first, "Take and eat"; then, "This is my body which was broken for you." First, "Drink ye all of this"; then, "This is my blood of the new covenant which is shed for many for the remission of sins."[1] I do not see any way to gather from Christ's words when and where the bread becomes his body or the cup his blood, except within the heart and soul of the one who receives them. The sacraments really *exhibit*, but from what we can gather from the text *are* not really, nor do they really *contain* in themselves, that grace which it pleases God to bestow with them or by them. Everyone confesses that the grace of baptism is poured into the soul, and that we receive grace by water even though the water itself neither contains nor turns into grace. Why, then, do men think that the grace of the eucharist must be in the eucharist itself before it can be in us who receive it? The fruit of the eucharist is our participation in the body and blood of Christ. There is no sentence in Holy Scripture that says we cannot be made partakers of his body and blood by this sacrament unless the sacrament itself first contains or is converted into them. "This is my body" and "This is my blood" are words of promise, and we all agree that Christ really and truly fulfills his

---

1. See Luke 22:19–20; Matthew 26:26–28; Mark 14:22–24.

promise in us by means of the sacrament. Why then do we vainly trouble ourselves with such fierce contentions about consubstantiation and transubstantiation, and whether or not the sacrament itself first possesses Christ or not? Whatever the answer might be, it can neither help nor hinder us. Our participation in Christ in this sacrament depends on the cooperation of his omnipotent power making it his body and blood for us. We do not need to greatly care or inquire whether or not he does this with some change to the elements such as they imagine.

(7.) Take what we all agree on, and then consider whether we should not leave the remaining questions to one side as superfluous, rather than insisting on them as necessary. All sides clearly confess:

First, that this sacrament is a true and real participation in Christ, who by it imparts his whole, entire person as the mystical head to every soul who receives him, and that those who receive are united or incorporated to Christ as mystical members of him, and of those whom he acknowledges as his own.

Second, that to those who thus receive his own person, Christ by this same sacrament gives his Holy Spirit to sanctify them just as the Spirit sanctifies him who is their head.

Third, that by this sacrament we freely, fully, and wholly have all the merit, power, and virtue of his sacrificed body and blood.

Fourth, that the effect of the sacrament in us is a real transmutation of our souls and bodies from sin to righteousness, from death and corruption to immortality and life.

Fifth, that since the corruptible and earthly nature of the sacramental elements makes them an unlikely instrument for such wonderful effects in man, we must rest wholly in the strong and glorious power of the one who can and will cause the bread and cup which he gives to truly be the thing he promises.

(8.) It seems wrong, therefore, that so many polemical treatises against the so-called "Sacramentarians"[2] all harp on two points: that the eucharist is not merely a bare sign or figure, and that the *effects* of his body and blood are not all we that receive in the sacrament. For anyone who has read the books and writing under attack can see that they plainly accept both of these points. These men do not interpret the words of Christ to mean that the name of his body only meant the "figure" of his

---

2. *Ed.* I.e., those aligned with the Swiss Reformation (e.g., the aforementioned Zwingli and Oecolampadius) on sacramental questions.

body, or that "is" only means "signifies" his blood. They grant that these holy mysteries, when properly received, instrumentally make us partakers of the grace of the body and blood which were given for the life of the world, and that they impart to us the very person of our Lord himself—whole, perfect, and entire—in a true and real though mystical manner.

(9.) All three opinions (the Reformed, Lutheran, and Roman) are agreed so far. But the strong conviction of the latter two that we literally, corporally, and orally chew the very substance of Christ's flesh and blood is an opinion that Scripture never expresses. Why then should they think themselves bound to believe it? In fact (to speak in the softest terms we can use), our Savior was greatly affronted when others conceived of eating his flesh in this way, and he told them directly that such eating his flesh would not profit them at all. For the words which he spoke were "spirit"—that is, they referenced a mystical participation which gives life [Jn. 6:63]. It seems unlikely that Christ's purpose was to make them reverse Marcionites as it were—that just as the Marcionites believed that Christ *seemed* to be a man but was not, Christ's disciples should believe that while Christ (to avoid offending them) would not *seem* to be giving them his flesh to eat in the way that horrified them, he was in fact doing so.

(10.) When those who have this opinion about Christ in the blessed sacrament try to explain how this substantial presence comes about, those who embrace "consubstantiation" begin with the union of Christ's deity and his manhood. They infer that the body of Christ has a power because of this union to present itself in all places, and from this "ubiquity" of his body they deduce its presence along with the sanctified bread and wine of our Lord's table. They argue that just as we call the Son of God a man because God and man are united in the person of Christ, so we call the bread his body because his body and blood are joined to the elements in the sacrament. They add that Christ's command to eat must mean that he had coupled the substance of his flesh and the substance of bread together, so that we should receive both together.

The other sort rightly shuns this Lutheran labyrinth, but they take a shortcut to the same tavern. For they imagine that transubstantiation follows the words of consecration through God's omnipotent power, at which point Christ's body and blood participate with the mere shapes of sacramental elements. So all three groups confess God's omnipotence. The "sacramentaries" believe that God's power accomplishes a transformation in us, as the other two groups also confess. The patrons of transubstantiation add that God all-powerfully changes one substance into another. The devotees of consubstantiation claim that his omnipotence accomplishes the kneading up of both substances into one lump.

(11.) But what did Christian antiquity teach on this question? First, since they knew that the power of this sacrament necessarily presupposes the truth of Christ's body and blood, they often used the sacrament as an example to demonstrate that Christ has the substance of man just as truly as of God, because in the sacrament we receive Christ and those graces which flow from him as a man. Tertullian, Irenaeus, and Theodoret all argue that if Christ is not both God and man, then the sacrament cannot have the meaning we all confess.[3] They also all clearly teach that Christ is *personally* and wholly present in the sacrament, even though a part of Christ is *corporally* absent from it. For Christ, assisting this heavenly banquet with his personal and true presence, adds by his own divine power a supernatural efficacy to the natural substance of the consecrated elements, and this addition to their

---

3. Tertullian, *Against Marcion* 4.40; Irenaeus, *Against Heresies* 5.1; Theodoret, *Dialogue, Unmixed,* in *Corpus Christianorum,* Series Graeca, 36:104.

nature changes them and makes them for us what they otherwise could not be. They become instruments for us that mystically yet truly, invisibly yet really bring about our communion or fellowship with the person of Jesus Christ, both as man and as God. By them, we participate in the fruit, grace, and efficacy of his body and blood, so that a kind of transubstantiation occurs within us—a true change of soul and body, an alteration from death to life. But we never see one of the ancient Fathers conceiving of or imagining anything other than a mystical participation in Christ's body and blood in the sacrament. Nor can a man assure himself in good conscience that their words concerning the change of the elements into the body and blood of Christ were meant to persuade the world either of a corporal consubstantiation between Christ and the sanctified and blessed elements before we receive them, or of a transubstantiation of the elements into the body and blood of Christ. Both consubstantiation and transubstantiation are so unnecessary for our mystical communion with Christ that we should not lightly suppose that the Fathers who hold simply to this mystical communion believed in any other change of sacramental elements than this spiritual communion required them to believe.

(12.) Considering all this, what should the virtuous and truth-loving mind think, the mind that seeks comfort from these holy mysteries, but lacks either the leisure, wit, or ability to tread the endless mazes of eucharistic controversy? It cannot do better than to say this: "This variety of judgments and opinions suggests that the debated points are obscure. But that which all sides have sifted, agreed on, and received as truth must be infallibly certain. Now, there are three interpretations of 'This is my body.' The first, which is the Lutherans' interpretation, is: 'This in itself before participation is really and truly the natural substance of my body, because of the coexistence of my omnipotent body with the sanctified element of bread.' The second, which is the popish interpretation, is: 'This in itself and before participation is the very true and natural substance of my body, by the power of that deity which abolishes the substance of bread and substitutes my body in its place at the words of consecration.' The third interpretation is this: 'This holy food, through the concurrence of divine power, is truly an instrumental cause of mystical participation for faithful receivers. Just as I make myself wholly theirs, so I give into their hands an actual possession of all such saving grace that my sacrificed body can yield and that their souls presently need. This is my body *for them* and *in them*.' This last interpretation has nothing in it except what the others all approve and acknowledge must be most true; nothing but what all sides confess that the words of

Christ enact; nothing but what the church of God has always thought necessary; nothing but what is alone sufficient for every Christian man to believe concerning the use and power of this sacrament; nothing, finally, but what the writings of all antiquity support and all Christian confessions agree on. And as truth never contradicts truth, the mind which rests itself on this is never troubled with the perplexities which the other two find from the great contradiction between their opinions and the true principles of reason grounded on experience, nature, and sense. And although they often seem to blow away their anxieties with boisterous courage and breath, whoever observes how they labor and sweat by subtlety of wit to show some agreement between their peculiar conceits and the general laws of nature, sees that they are struggling with something they cannot fully master.

"We also see that when they debate 'consubstantiation' or 'transubstantiation' their writing is hungry and unpleasant, tedious and laborious, heartless and till now fruitless, while when we read or hear both ancient and modern divines on those points where all speak unanimously (regardless of their opinions on the controversial points), their words are heavenly and as sweet as the honeycomb, their tongues melodiously tuned instruments, their sentences full only of consolation and joy. Is this not itself almost a voice from heaven showing us

the safest position to hold? He who said of one sacrament 'Wash and be clean,' has said of the other
'Eat and live.' If the poor distressed woman who
came to Christ for health could tell herself, even
without such a direct promise, 'If only I may touch
his garment, I shall be made well' [Mt. 9:21], why
should we argue about the manner by which life
comes through bread? Our duty is simply to take
what is offered, and to rest assured that if we can
but eat we are safe.

"When I see some small and scarcely discern-
ible grain or seed which nature promises shall become a tree, or when some skillful artificer frames
something exquisite from that tree, I behold the
result; I do not question how either the tree or the
work of art was made. Shall I simply credit nature
in natural things, and trust art in artificial things,
never raising doubts or scruples, but in something
above both art and nature refuse to believe the author of both unless he acquaints me with his ways
and lays the secrets of his skill before me? When
God himself speaks things which (either because
of their height and sublimity or the hiddenness of
their performance) we cannot comprehend, and of
which we can be safely ignorant, it can be no disgrace to confess our ignorance. Those who love piety will, so far as it lies in them, know all things that
God commands, but especially those duties of service which they owe to God. As regards God's dark

and hidden works, they prefer a humble simplicity of faith rather than a knowledge that curiously sifts what it should adore, and disputes too boldly of things which the wit of man cannot search, chilling most often all warmth of zeal, and endangering the soundness of belief. Let it be enough for me, then, when I present myself at the Lord's table, to know *what* I receive from him there, without searching or inquiring *how* Christ performs his promise. Let disputes and questions—the enemies of piety and hindrances to true devotion, which on this matter have been too patiently heard—take their rest. Let curious and sharp-witted men beat their heads about what questions they like. The very letter of the Word of Christ gives plain assurance that these mysteries fasten us as nails to his very cross, that by them we draw out even the efficacy, power, and virtue of the blood from his gored side, that we there dip our tongues in the wounds of our Redeemer and are dyed red both within and without, that our hunger is satisfied and our thirst forever quenched. He whose soul possesses this paschal lamb and rejoices in the strength of this new wine feels wonderful things, sees great things, and utters unheard-of things. This bread contains more than the substance which our eyes behold. This cup, hallowed with a solemn benediction, avails to the endless life and health of both soul and body, for it serves both as a medicine to heal our infirmities and purge our sins, and as a sacrifice of thanksgiving. It sanctifies what it touches, enlightens us with belief, and truly conforms us to the image of Jesus Christ. It matters not what these elements are in themselves; it is enough that to me who receive them they are the body and blood of Christ. His promise suffices as a witness of this; he knows how to accomplish his words. Why should any thought possess the mind of the faithful communicant but this: 'Oh my God, you are true. O my soul, you are happy'?"

(13.) Therefore, however men's opinions otherwise vary regarding baptism and the Lord's supper, we may conclude, with the consent of the whole Christian world, that they are necessary—the first to initiate or begin, the second to consummate or perfect our life in Christ.

MORE FROM DAVENANT PRESS

INTRODUCTION TO PROTESTANT THEOLOGY
Reformation Theology: A Reader of Primary Sources with Introductions

Grace Worth Fighting For: Recapturing the Vision of God's Grace in the Canons of Dordt

Synopsis of a Purer Theology

PETER MARTYR VERMIGLI LIBRARY
Dialogue on the Two Natures in Christ

Philosophical Works: On the Relation of Philosophy to Theology

The Oxford Treatise and Disputation on the Eucharist, 1549

Predestination and Justification: Two Theological Loci

VERMIGLI'S COMMON PLACES
On Original Sin (Vol. 1)

On Free Will and the Law (Vol. 2)

LIBRARY OF EARLY ENGLISH PROTESTANTISM
James Ussher and a Reformed Episcopal Church: Sermons and Treatises on Ecclesiology

The Apology of the Church of England

Jurisdiction Regal, Episcopal, Papal

Radicalism: When Reform Becomes Revolution

ABOUT THE
DAVENANT INSTITUTE

The Davenant Institute supports the renewal of Christian wisdom for the contemporary church. It seeks to sponsor historical scholarship at the intersection of the church and academy, build networks of friendship and collaboration within the Reformed and evangelical world, and equip the saints with time-tested resources for faithful public witness.

We are a nonprofit organization supported by your tax-deductible gifts. Learn more about us, and donate, at www.davenantinstitute.org

46461645R00108